Succeed as a musician without sacrificing your faith

ALLEN C. PAUL

God and Gigs

Copyright © 2016 by Allen C. Paul
All rights reserved. This book or any portion thereof may not be reproduced or used in any manner whatsoever without the express written permission of the publisher except for the use of brief quotations in a book review.

Printed in the United States of America
First Printing, 2016
ISBN 978-0-9972703-0-3
www.GodandGigs.com

All Scripture quotations, unless otherwise indicated, are taken from the Holy Bible, New International Version®, NIV®. Copyright ©1973, 1978, 1984, 2011 by Biblica, Inc.™ Used by permission of Zondervan. All rights reserved worldwide. www.zondervan.com The "NIV" and "New International Version" are trademarks registered in the United States Patent and Trademark Office by Biblica, Inc.™

Scripture quotations marked NLT are taken from the Holy Bible, New Living Translation, copyright ©1996, 2004, 2007, 2013, 2015 by Tyndale House Foundation. Used by permission of Tyndale House Publishers, Inc., Carol Stream, Illinois 60188. All rights reserved.

Scripture quotations marked NASB are taken from the NEW AMERICAN STANDARD BIBLE(R), Copyright (C) 1960,1962,1963,1968,1971,1972,1973,1975,1977,1995 by The Lockman Foundation. Used by permission.

Scripture quotations from THE MESSAGE. Copyright © by Eugene H. Peterson 1993, 1994, 1995, 1996, 2000, 2001, 2002. Used by permission of NavPress. All rights reserved. Represented by Tyndale House Publishers, Inc.

Dedication

To my parents,
Dr. Marcus and Reita Paul, for giving me the gifts
of faith, music, and the love of learning.

ACKNOWLEDGMENTS

The problem with making a list of people to thank is that the list will never be complete. It's impossible to list the hundreds of supporters, musicians, and friends that have impacted my life, and therefore inspired this book. All I can do is attempt to acknowledge a few of them, and hope that all of you realize how much I value each and every contributor to this project.

To my amazing wife, Lia, and our three kids, Chris, Marcus, and Naomi, thanks for allowing your husband and father to disappear into literary exile day after day. Your love and support have truly made this journey worth it. You are the reasons why I continue to strive for excellence, because you all deserve my best every day. Oh, and you are all hilarious too.

To my amazing church family, Metro Life Church, and my pastors Steve and Mary Alessi, thank you for giving me the confidence, guidance, and spiritual covering to be both a worshipper and an artist; never making me choose between the two. Your example has made my life richer and more meaningful, because I finally felt comfortable in my calling. Thanks also to those in other ministries I've served in throughout the years, most notably Jehovah Lutheran Church and Second Baptist Church, both of which were instrumental in my development as a musician and worship leader.

To all the musicians, singers, artists, engineers, and audiences that have in some way contributed to this book, I cannot thank you enough. It was your support that allowed me to enjoy and sustain this career. I must stop and thank every musician that lent a quote, interview, email, or kind word toward this book. It really is about you more than it is about anything else. The light of your integrity, faith and belief in this occupation's ability to bless people has illuminated my understanding of the power we hold in our hands every time we perform.

I must take the risk of overlooking some folks in order to thank others, so let me just mention a few major inspirations that started this journey with me. Khristian Dentley, you spurred me on both musically and spiritually with your great charm, authenticity, and enthusiasm. Thank you so much! Trent Phillips, you were one of the first musicians that inspired me to make this project more than a pamphlet handed out at a workshop. Thank you for lending your prodigious wisdom. Parris Bowens, you came in and took this project to a whole new level with your insight and encouragement. To all of the local musicians (too many to name) that provided support – this book is my way of honoring your work and your commitment to excellence.

ALLEN C. PAUL

To all the people that contributed to the God and Gigs fundraiser, your financial contribution made the book you are holding in your hands possible. Thank you for believing in this project and making a tangible investment into it. I hope you're satisfied with the results. I must give some special thanks to these "Hall of Fame" contributors who made sizable contributions:

Steve Alessi
Macky Diaz
Lillie Edwards
Joel Cristela Espinoza
Mory Martinez
Melton Mustafa
Charles W. Phipps, Sr.
Marcus A. Paul
Reita Paul
David Roman
Mike and Kristie Valdez

I owe a huge debt of gratitude to the editors and writers who guided me through this brand new world of publishing. Katrina Holder (aka Poettis), it was your insightful eye and unflinching attention to detail that brought much needed focus to this book. Thank you for keeping me on track! Lee Stranahan, you are a dear brother whose clarity and honesty I value highly. Thank you for your attentive notes and encouragement. To Carol Banks Weber, your consistent support of this project acted as wind in my sails. Other writers who taught me the ins and out of the book business have asked to remain anonymous, but without their help, I never would have gotten a word into print.

You may wonder why I haven't thanked God. The reason is this: if you do not sense my gratefulness to him in every word that follows, then I have done a very poor job of writing.

CONTENTS

INTRODUCTION	7
PART I: YOUR CONNECTIONS	23
Chapter 1: Stay Connected To Church	24
Chapter 2: Stay Connected To Your Spouse	38
Chapter 3: Stay Connected To Your Children	52
Chapter 4: Stay Connected To God	65
PART II: YOUR CAREER	81
Chapter 5: Establish Your Priorities	82
Chapter 6: Respect The Business	107
Chapter 7: Visualize Your Goals	128
Chapter 8: Invest In Your Skill	147
PART III: YOUR CALLING	159
Chapter 9: Challenged Yourself To Grow	160
Chapter 10: Evangelize Through Your Gift	174
Appendix	192

INTRODUCTION

"The world never let a man bless it but it first fought him."

-Henry Ward Beecher

It's one of *those* Saturday nights. You're playing a gig that promised to be easy, but it turned out to be a nightmare. One person is playing the bridge, someone else is playing the chorus, and the leader of the band is in his own world, playing a totally unrelated groove that sounds like a horrible combination of polka and reggae. Not to mention, it's almost 1 AM in a casino lounge, thick with the caustic scent of cigars and the cacophony of slot machine music constantly in the background. A few intoxicated bar regulars are swimming in their drinks in front of you, but they're totally ignoring the band. Other blank faced customers seated at the slot machines glance at the mess on stage every now and again, only to turn back around to pull the lever and stare at the spinning cherries and sevens. You're amazed that they don't even notice how bad it sounds. On top of all of this, you are supposed to be ready for the praise and worship sound check at church tomorrow morning.

Your heart is heavy and your mind is anywhere but on the music as the band continues to miss chords on the chorus. You feel lost, unfulfilled, and unsure of whether or not this is where you are supposed to be. You're talented and you want to play music for a living, not just on Sunday mornings. You also don't enjoy playing gigs where you're exposed to behaviors that you just don't agree with. The question that's constantly at the back of your mind is, Am I pleasing God when I perform this kind of music?"

What's more, you are imagining the disapproving, sour-faced looks you'll get in the morning from the church members that saw your Facebook post announcing the scheduled gig. They act as if they weren't probably at similar places last night themselves; but that's beside the point.

If you've ever experienced a situation where your faith and your music career created a conflict, this book is for you.

If you're still with me, my guess is that you fit into one of three categories:

1. A musician that plays in a church or ministry;

2. A musician that plays or sings professionally or as a freelancer in popular music performances – aka "gigs";

3. A musician that constantly deals with conflicts between number one and number two.

If any of these describe you, I hope you'll continue reading. You may have thought no one else understood the dilemmas you face. You may think that the conflict I mentioned is just something you have to live with. My goal is to convince you that you're not alone, and that there are ways to survive the challenge and become a happy and successful musician, no matter where you play your music.

WHAT THIS BOOK WILL NOT TELL YOU

We must start with two questions that will NOT be the focus of this book. I often hear these questions from critics of musicians that play gigs, but they are distractions from the real-life issues we face.

Question #1: "Should church musicians perform in secular environments?"

Some Christians claim that musicians are excluded from using their gifts anywhere but within the church walls. This premise would take a whole book to discuss. Because it often dominates the discourse, let's clear it up quickly. First, let's define the word "secular". This word describes things that have no religious or spiritual value. The problem with using the term secular is that it divides our lives into two parts: things that are connected to God and things that are not. That's a flawed view of the real world. God is connected, in some way, to everything we do. There is no facet of human existence that can be segregated from Christ's influence.

Should Christian doctors only treat Christian patients? Is it possible for Christian contractors to only build Christian homes? Hardly. In the same way, it doesn't make sense for Christian musicians to use their skills solely in Christian environments.

The legendary Dr. Charles Swindoll of "Insight for Living" said it this way:

"When you have a sense of calling, whether it's to be a musician, soloist, artist, in one of the technical fields, or a plumber, there is something deep and enriching when you realize it isn't just a casual choice, it's a divine calling. It's not limited to vocational Christian service by any means. "[d]

For the sake of clarity, I will sometimes use *secular* to describe music that isn't explicitly Christian, but I prefer to use the term *popular* to describe the modern music industry. This definition includes any genre of music that is produced commercially, not just pop.

Are there times when Christian musicians dedicate their gifts exclusively to ministry? Absolutely! I served as a full-time minister of music for three years. During that time, I did not

---

[1]

http://www.toledoblade.com/Religion/2012/02/25/Radio-host-shares-his-experience-in-new-book.html play any outside gigs other than wedding receptions. However, this does not mean every Christian musician is called to full-time ministry. We use our talents to serve God, but also to provide ourselves with income.

Before we begin this discussion, you should understand that God gives us the freedom to exercise our talents both inside and outside the church. If you're struggling with this notion, pay close attention to the "Conversations with the Pros" interviews throughout the book. You'll gain valuable insights from successful musicians that have conquered the supposed conflicts between church and the gig.

Question #2: "Shouldn't churches pay musicians enough so they don't have to play gigs?"

While I wish every church had a music budget big enough to hire full-time staff musicians, this isn't realistic. Despite the growth and professionalization of music ministry, hiring full-time musicians is not feasible for many churches and ministries. I do believe that music ministry is a profession that deserves compensation, but I can't tell you how much a church musician should be paid. That is a question for each musician, church board, and pastor to decide on an independent basis. Perhaps by reading this material, church leaders and pastors will better understand what their musicians go through in order to maintain their career.

Allen C. Paul

WHAT THIS BOOK WILL TELL YOU

I'm interested in helping you to avoid the struggles you face in both the music ministry and the popular music industry. If you have worked for any length of time in either field, you know how it feels to be torn between the two. Most likely, you've uttered one or more of these phrases:

"I had a paying gig at the same time that the church had a service I wasn't being paid for…I didn't know what to do. Am I being selfish because I need the money?"

"My band is always playing late night Saturday gigs, making me tired on Sunday mornings, but they say we have to do it to be in front of the big crowds."

"I practice more for my gigs than my church rehearsals, but we always play the same music at church, so I don't feel motivated to practice for that."

"I'm so frustrated by my lack of ability. I'm stuck, and no one will help me at church or when I rehearse with the band."

Hear me when I say, you're not alone. I asked myself these questions daily as I struggled to balance my desire to serve in the church with my professional responsibilities and in the music industry. It seemed like there was nothing available to help me wrestle with these competing interests. That is, until I found a passage in the Bible that helped me reconcile my faith with my love of music. Allow me to break this passage down so that it can encourage you as well.

A BIBLICAL MODEL

In Nehemiah 13, the Israelites have returned to Jerusalem from captivity in Babylon, led by Nehemiah, and have rebuilt their city, despite a lot of opposition. However, Nehemiah has to return to his post in Babylon and leaves the control of the city to the priests and elders. When he returns to Jerusalem some time later, he finds a sad state of affairs. The Levites, a group of musicians, singers, and priests, who were dedicated to serving in the temple and were supposed to be supported by the temple offerings, hadn't received the financial support they were promised. As a result, all the workers had left the temple and returned "to their fields" (vs. 10). In other words, they returned to the place where they could earn a living when not serving in the temple.

While the historical Levites led Israel in worship and maintained the temple, today's churchgoers generally associate Levites with musicians. Musicians that serve in the modern church are equivalent to the Levites because they are an integral part of our worship services. For a deeper understanding of the Levitical priesthood, I suggest doing a Bible word study.

It's true that the Levites' exit from the temple was due to the mismanagement of their pay, but I do not believe that modern musicians work outside the church only because they aren't paid enough. In fact, it is clear from scripture that the Levites were only allowed to serve for a limited time in the temple. So what did the Levite musicians do when they were released from ministry? Did they stop composing songs or put away their instruments? Any musician knows that it's against their nature to simply give up playing. While not explicitly addressed in scripture, it's reasonable to assume that they continued performing, writing, and teaching music. In other words, they continued to do what they were gifted to do wherever they were – whether in God's house or in their own houses and towns.

This is why I believe God has musicians, dancers and other artists that cannot be confined to ministry within local congregations. Sure, you can serve God with your talents in the church, but that's not necessarily where your talents are destined to stay. Your gifts can be used to glorify God everywhere you go. The issue is not whether you should be in the field; rather, it is how you can maximize your influence in the outside world while maintaining your foundation of faith.

Make no mistake; **it is possible** to have a real and consistent Christian walk while actively working in the music industry, but it will be a challenge. No matter where or what you perform, there will be always be the potential for conflict between your career and your faith. I know this first hand.

MY STORY

My music career began where many of us musicians get our start – in the church. As a teen in our small Lutheran ministry, I played organ alongside my mother, who was the head pianist. I was chosen to become the director of the youth choir. Of course, the youth choir didn't want to sing 'Pass Me Not, O Gentle Savior' as Kirk Franklin and other gospel artists were beginning to electrify the gospel industry with hip R&B styled songs. My mom wasn't comfortable playing those songs. Ironically, I wasn't comfortable with modern gospel either. My exposure to gospel music was limited, and I struggled to master the style. I remember the first time we tried to get the congregation to clap along. It was as if we had offered them vinegar for communion. Even at this early stage of my career, I was beginning to learn that churches don't always encourage musicians to develop new skills and styles.

When I graduated from high school, I was confident of two things; one, music would be my chosen profession, and two, I wanted to be in a band. I entered the University of Miami as a classical pianist and music education major, but quickly found jazz a much better fit for my sensibilities. As I progressed, I began playing dinner music in restaurants and R & B covers with friends in the jazz school. Our little R&B band gained a few fans on campus as we performed at local restaurants and bars. Having never played gigs before, I was overwhelmed by the experience. I enjoyed the loud cheers of the audience, the excitement of the stage and the euphoria of amazing musical moments. However, I also soon learned the drawbacks of the gig life: dragging equipment blocks at a time; arguing with promoters and lazy sound engineers; packing up rusty U-Haul trailers; riding in stuffy, rented vans for hours on dark highways, praying that the drummer would stay awake when it was his turn to drive. Not surprisingly, none of our members wanted to live that life while promoting a funk band in an industry where only rap, hip-hop and pop artists seemed to survive. The band broke up and I moved on with my collegiate studies, assuming that my gig-playing days were essentially over.

Around this time, I got my first church job playing for a youth choir. My commitment was limited to showing up on Sundays and for rehearsals. I wasn't planning to join the church, nor did I want to. It was a simply a convenient job for a starving college musician. However, while I thought I was simply fulfilling my church responsibilities, God was working on my heart and altering my goals. When I graduated and began teaching music, I found myself thinking about choir practice and working on Sunday service plans in between classes. While I loved exploring music with my students, I felt like I wasn't maximizing my abilities as a public school teacher. After a lot of prayer and thought, I resigned from my elementary music teaching position to focus on raising my children and developing the music ministry at my church. A few years later, I was promoted to minister of music. I felt I had reached my ultimate purpose as a Christian musician: serving in a ministry full-time. It turned out that God wasn't done changing my plans.

I served in my position diligently. I gave my all to the church leadership, music ministry and congregation, trying to be the best leader I could. However, running a music ministry isn't just about being a great musician or a great leader. It requires a keen awareness of the realities of the modern music industry, and I was ignorant of everything that entailed. We hired young, talented musicians for our worship band, but I quickly learned that their gigs often conflicted with church services. I knew the budget we offered our musicians couldn't compete or compare with the amounts they could make by working outside the church. Of course, many in the church leadership believed that musicians only cared about money. As a musician myself, I felt conflicted. How could I insist that my staff give up higher paying gigs when I knew it was impossible for them to survive on their church income alone?

While I struggled to manage our staff musicians, I was also frustrated with my own development. I was getting better as a gospel pianist, but other facets of my playing weren't being utilized. Outlets for musical growth were scarce, especially since I didn't play outside gigs anymore. I was stuck. My family was experiencing the stress and strain of upholding the public persona of a perfect ministry family while, internally, we were struggling emotionally and financially.

After a year of prayer and seeking God's direction, I resigned from my position as minister of music and gave up what was potentially a promotion to associate pastor. You would think, after a year of preparation, I would have been able to plan a smooth transition into a new position or church. If only that were true. I left my position with no idea what to do next. All I knew was that God had given me instructions, and he'd have to show me the way forward. And, just like he sometimes does, God waited till I exhausted all other options before proving himself faithful. Three days after resigning, I received a call from a neighbor who was on the praise team of my current church. Two weeks later, I was on staff, playing for church services in a new ministry – but with a key difference. I could no longer depend on full-time employment from the church. I had to start using my other skills and abilities to provide for my family.

Around the same time, I was invited to play at a couple of jazz jam sessions. It had been years since I played for an event that wasn't church-related. After some practice and networking, I began supplementing my income by playing at restaurants. Even though I wasn't making a lot of money, these performances ignited the passion I used to have for music performance. It confirmed in my heart that God wanted me to be more than just a Sunday morning musician. He wanted me to be a Monday thru Saturday night one as well. I was reaching people beyond the four walls of the church with my gifts, yet still blessing the God that gave them to me.

I tell you my story because I want you to know that I understand your struggle. I've been the typical musician operating in several different roles; the one hauling gear out of the smoke-filled blues club at 2 AM, and the one leading prayer with the praise team before early morning service. I'm no stranger to all-day rehearsals for Sunday School Christmas concerts with crying toddlers, frustrated directors, and fretting church volunteers, nor to couples gyrating on the dance floor as I played Chaka Khan covers and sparkling disco lights spun. I can recall hyped crowds at wedding receptions jumping in unison to chorus after chorus of "Party Rock", but I also fondly remember the rush of the Holy Spirit's power as a crowd of worshippers, hands raised, some crying, some kneeling, sang out the refrain "Your Presence is Heaven to

Me" for thirty minutes straight . God has blessed me as I've served him in church, and he's also blessed me with work outside of the church. This is what I hope you'll understand more and more as you read this book. You can fully express your creativity and bring joy to audiences while remaining a committed believer in Christ.

YOU'RE NOT ALONE

From my personal experience, I estimate that the majority of professional church musicians are not exclusively performing in the church. They play at receptions, clubs, and restaurants, teach lessons, tour with other artists and perform on their own as they make either a part-time or full-time career out of their music. Although this may not be a well-known fact inside the church, it shouldn't be surprising. Many churches cannot afford full-time musicians, and musicians in general tend to have their eggs in more than just one basket. The more talent a musician has, the more likely that his or her abilities are not only utilized on Sundays, but also throughout the week.

If you are a musician that plays for a church and also plays gigs professionally, then you have to face certain realities.

1. You will have scheduling conflicts. As a busy musician, conflicts between church functions and gigs or rehearsals are inevitable. Many musicians base their choices on financial considerations, but in my opinion, that's not the only priority you should consider.

2. You will find that you have different roles in church and on your gig. While there may be similarities between the music of the church and music as entertainment, there are huge differences in how they should be approached professionally. While the roles differ greatly, you can be effective, both on the bandstand and behind the pulpit.

3. Your decisions to play secular music will be questioned. There are Christians who stigmatize mainstream music, even if the songs promote married love, non-violence, or any other inspirational subject. If Jesus is not mentioned somewhere in the lyrics, someone will accuse you of selling out. If you allow these critics to determine your choices, you will forfeit a valuable part of your God-given influence as a Christian artist. Neither the world nor short-sighted believers should dictate the boundaries of your artistic expression. Your gift and art belong to God alone, and his Spirit can guide you toward what honors him and away from the traps you must avoid. It is possible to embrace your freedom and calling as a Christian musician in our mainstream culture.

Allen C. Paul

THE S.E.R.V.I.C.E. MODEL

Like you, I constantly deal with issues involving my faith and my professional music career. One morning, as I was thinking about these things, God dropped an acronym in my spirit. I believe these seven steps provide a roadmap to success for any Christian musician. It is called the S.E.R.V.I.C.E. model.

S – Stay connected.
E – Establish your priorities.
R – Respect the business.
V – Visualize your goals.
I – Invest in your craft.
C – Challenge yourself to grow.
E – Evangelize through your gift.

If you follow these seven action steps, you can successfully manage the concerns of performing music professionally, both for evangelism and for entertainment. A S.E.R.V.I.C.E. attitude can improve your prospects as a gigging musician and, more importantly, protect and accentuate your faith and influence as a Christian musician and artist. The SERVICE steps can be divided into three parts: your **connections**, your **career**, and your **calling**. Put them together, and you have a complete view of how to succeed as a musician of faith.

Part I:
Your Connections

Chapter One

Stay Connected to Church

"You can be committed to Church but not committed to Christ, but you cannot be committed to Christ and not committed to church."

-Joel Osteen

"...and that's when I said to the pastor, 'Three day revival? You MUST be joking. Good luck finding another drummer!' And I walked out!"

Dee smiled and leaned against the wall outside the sanctuary, where the rest of the band gathered after Sunday service. An accomplished drummer, Dee had played in this church for a year and was known for moving around to any ministry that would pay a higher salary. Being a musician in high demand among artists and groups caused Dee to walk around with a sense of entitlement. The rest of the band merely tolerated this attitude. They didn't appreciate the frequent ego trips, but they weren't looking forward to another musician search. The pastor of the church was happy with the concert-like atmosphere the music ministry brought every Sunday.

Dee looked around at the band and asked, "So why are we still here? You want to grab some lunch?"

One by one, each band member explained that they had to remain for a meeting after church. They all served in various teams in that ministry.

Dee laughed sarcastically. "That's the problem! You all got suckered in to this 'membership' thing. Not me. I'm a free agent. No church is gonna own all my time."

With that, Dee drove away – not knowing, within minutes, a serious car accident would result in serious injuries and a long recovery. After contacting family, the first call Dee made was to the band members to ask for their prayers. Besides, they were the only church members Dee knew by name.

Sadly, Dee had to face a trial to realize that church is more than a place to make a paycheck. It is an extended family.

.

Allen C. Paul

THE CONNECTIONS THAT MATTER

Music is all about connections. Every musician learns this truth quickly as they join a band, work with an instructor, or participate in a studio session. Even if you are performing alone, you are still dependent on other people: the audience, the sound engineer, the owner of the venue, the promoter, etc. There is never a time that you can remain on a virtual island without needing others to help you succeed.

We find this principle applied in scripture as well. Repeatedly, the word of God emphasizes the power of teamwork. Solomon says, "A person standing alone can be attacked and defeated, but two can stand back-to-back and conquer. Three are even better, for a triple-braided cord is not easily broken" (Ecc 4:12 NLT). Even God recognized the power of unity in Genesis. 'Look!' He said. 'The people are united, and they all speak the same language. After this, nothing they set out to do will be impossible for them'" (Gen 11:6 NLT).

Being a musician requires some times of solitude. We are alone with our instruments, computers, and notepads for hours, sweating over tricky techniques or trying to find the perfect phrase for a new song. However, to become complete as artists, we eventually have to bring others into our lives. We all want to work with other great musicians, but the important relationships go deeper than music. To be a successful Christian musician, you need three relationships to remain strong and vibrant. You need your relationships with the *church,* your *family,* and *God.*

These three relationships are critical to long-term success and balance in our lives. Unfortunately, we often neglect these relationships, and soon the effects of disconnection become evident. If we're not careful, we risk becoming isolated and disillusioned. Without support in these three areas, even a successful music career will not satisfy the spiritual and emotional needs that every artist requires to stay productive and creative.

WHY YOU CAN'T NEGLECT YOUR CHURCH CONNECTION

For starters, the relationship with the church is a highly sensitive one for many musicians. Remember our fictional situation with Dee, the hired-gun musician who never connected with the church? The conclusion was a bit extreme, yes, but the sentiments that Dee expressed are shared by many musicians who are wary about joining a ministry. Here are some other quotes you might hear from musicians who are not members of the church they currently serve.

"They'll expect me to volunteer."

"Once I join, they'll expect me to be there all the time."

"Churches are unfriendly to musicians that gig."

All of these excuses avoid the central issue. If you are a Christian, you should be a member of a church. Your career as a musician doesn't change this fact. A better, more honest question is, "Can a musician be a member of a church without being disconnected or misunderstood?" The answer is Yes.

There are no perfect churches, just as there are no perfect musicians. Staying connected is not about being part of a perfect church. It is about growing, maturing, and deepening your faith openly and transparently. If you can't be yourself in a community of Christians, you'll find it hard to be authentic on stage and in public. However, if you truly engage and connect with a local healthy church family, you'll find the *stability* and *accountability* you need to survive and thrive in all of your endeavors.

STABILITY

The musical lifestyle is full of constant change. We may be in one band one day, and in an entirely different band the next day. Every situation brings new challenges and requires flexibility. We adjust our schedules, our living arrangements, and sometimes even our appearance for the sake of our music. With all these changes, we need influences that are consistent. The local church can be that source of stability. However, you can't find stability in a church if you don't first choose to commit to being a part of a local ministry.

This doesn't just mean becoming a member. A member of a church has a certificate of membership, or perhaps has their name on the church bulletin or roster. However, membership doesn't provide connection. You must go beyond membership and become a part of the church family. If you aren't sure what this means, think of how a healthy family operates. They share everything, laugh and play together, cry and struggle together, and most importantly, express their love for each other. That's what a church family should be doing for each other, and you won't find stability in a church unless you are helping to make that picture of true Christian fellowship a reality.

How do you move past membership into real family connection? The key is found in Psalms 92:13 *They that are planted in the house of the LORD shall flourish in the courts of our God.* (ESV) In other words, you have to put your roots in the soil of your ministry. Get to know the people in your congregation. Show up to events outside of music rehearsals and Sunday services. Be involved! If you are on the staff of your church, this is extremely important. It's not enough to be on stage during worship services. You're a fellow worshipper that serves the same God and shares the same struggles as those in your church community. If you are on the staff of one church but a member of another, it's even more important to make the effort to connect with your home ministry in other ways.

The emphasis has been on what you should do to connect with a healthy church family, but not all churches share this mentality. What do you do if your church relationship doesn't resemble a healthy family? What if it looks more like an episode of Divorce Court?

It's sad but true. Churches are not always safe places for relationships. Just as the family members we love the most can cause us the most pain, our ministries can bring us hardship and heartache as well. The Church has divine purpose, but it is populated by damaged people who will inevitably make mistakes. Don't let that be your excuse for turning your back on the church though. When conflicts arise, work to promote reconciliation, as scripture instructs us in Romans 12:18: *If it is possible, as far as it depends on you, live at peace with everyone.* If your relationship with a church comes to an end, don't let it be because of a breakdown of communication. Do your best to honor those that labored with you, and leave knowing that you have given your best to your former church. This attitude sets you up for God's blessing in your next assignment.

ACCOUNTABILITY

Another area that plagues musicians without a real church connection is a lack of accountability. When we think of accountability, many of us imagine a crotchety old church mother wagging a finger in our faces, chastising us for not saying grace before eating. That isn't true spiritual accountability. It actually happens when a group of believers agree to encourage and remind each other of their personal commitments to God. This takes place in a variety of ways.

Some churches promote healthy accountability by promoting weekly small groups, while others have men's or women's ministries, a prayer teleconferences, or text lines. Whatever method is used, a system of accountability helps you check your motives, your attitudes, and your decisions in the presence of other Christians that you can trust.

Ideally, accountability groups and our families complement each other to encourage our walk with God. If we have un-churched family members, we may need these groups even more. Either way, they are a great benefit to the Christian musician. There are some struggles that we need to share with another trusted friend before they can be addressed in our families. When areas of indecision or unhealthy habits arise, a Spirit-led accountability group can be the difference between a wise, God-honoring choice and one that leads to pain and heartache.

As we work on our gigs and tours, we are bombarded with temptations that can shipwreck our faith. In order to maintain our standards and our witness, there has to be some self-evaluation. I strongly encourage musicians to form accountability groups for this reason. A strong group of Christian musicians can anticipate the kind of spiritual hazards that we face on a nightly basis and can call out each other when they see their brothers and sisters slipping into dangerous territory.

I am blessed to have close friends and fellow Christian musicians who help me stay true to my faith. They've pulled me aside and confronted me when I've been wrong relationally or spiritually, and they've prayed for me and pushed me to be a better man. Every time we sit down for coffee or enjoy a meal together, they encourage me to win the battles I face as an artist in the marketplace. Without these brothers in my life, I would not be enjoying the blessings I have today as a husband, father, and musician. I can't implore you enough to seek out and encourage these kinds of relationships in your church. They will prove invaluable in your life and career.

Along with being accountable to our fellow church members, we must also be accountable to a local pastor or church leader. In the absence of a spiritual leader, even the strongest believer will become weak and spiritually malnourished. Some Christians attempt to replace the role of a pastor by getting all their biblical teaching from popular preachers on the internet, radio, and television. This strategy is like a child running to a different neighbor's house every night and sitting at their tables for dinner while neglecting the meals his mother cooks at home. Those at home know your needs better than anyone else. In the same way, while other media-based ministries can be helpful resources, the pastors and leaders in your local church are the ones God expects you to look to for guidance.

The world already understands the need for accountability. Whether religious or not, people all over the world look for leaders that will guide, counsel, and advise them. For example, Oprah Winfrey has been drawing thousands to arenas and millions to her television shows. Her followers seek her perspective and wisdom to order improve their lives. Thankfully, Christian leaders are also taking the lead as voices of guidance to our cultural icons. For example, Kanye West, one of the most self-assured (for lack of a better term) stars of this generation, routinely visits with one of South Florida's prominent pastors for guidance and counsel. If Kanye is willing to listen to a pastor's advice, then certainly Christian musicians should be seeking the leadership of trusted pastors in our local congregations.

Allen C. Paul

WHAT TO LOOK FOR IN A CHURCH

If you have already found a church home, continue to cultivate a strong relationship with your ministry. If you have yet to find your church home, there are some key things you should look for. First of all, find a healthy church that preaches the unaltered gospel of Jesus Christ as Lord and Savior and teaches the Bible in its entirety. Denominations can differ in their worship styles and particular teachings, but don't let denominational differences stop you from joining a great church, unless those practices conflict with biblical truth. Secondly, check out the culture of the church. A healthy church promotes love of God and love for people. Are the members happy, balanced, God-loving, and open to new people and friends? Are the pastors and leaders walking the talk in their own lives and in the lives of their families? While every church will have struggles and imperfections, the overall culture of the church should reflect one of grace, forgiveness, and a commitment to reaching the world for Christ.

If those qualifications are met, examine the church's view of your profession. Do they understand your calling to play music both within and outside the church? Do they see music as being owned by the church or owned by God? Does the pastor have a heart for artists and the role artists play in the culture? If the pastor is a musician, as many pastors are formerly or currently involved in music ministry, is he or she willing to nurture other musicians? You want to be in a place that encourages, not diminishes, the work God has called you to do. At my church in Miami, I'm blessed with pastors who are keenly aware of how music and the arts influence culture. Instead of keeping our staff in a Christian cocoon, they encourage our team members to use their gifts beyond the church walls. This freedom is a lifeline to a musician like me who once struggled with the notion of being called to a profession outside of full-time ministry.

In conclusion, pray, talk to other Christian musicians, and take your time as you consider joining a church. It's a big decision. With prayer, I believe God will lead you to the place where you'll be able to find comfort, challenge and encouragement. Even if your employment and your membership are in different ministries, maintain your church connection to the best of your ability. No matter what your situation, having a healthy relationship with a home church will provide the stability and accountability that you need.

THE CHURCH IS NOT THE ENEMY

It may be tempting to keep your distance from a ministry because it keeps things from getting complicated. Relationships are hard work. It takes time and effort to be visible, present, and active in a ministry outside of the musical responsibilities. Many musicians seem to balk at this step, especially if they are already employed by the church. They worry that commitment to a church is a doorway to having their talents misused or taken for granted.

Unfortunately, sometimes that fear is legitimate. In some churches, a staff musician that becomes a member is suddenly considered a volunteer. Responsibilities that were once considered part of their job are now considered part of their duties as a member, and no longer compensated. The volunteer mentality has convinced many a musician to avoid committing or connecting to a church out of fear of being abused professionally. Disconnection, however, will cost you more than you know.

Remember, just because a church has mistreated you in the past does not mean every church is out to get you. There may be misunderstandings and moments of conflict in your ministry. Stay connected anyway. The local church brings together imperfect people to worship a perfect God. He then uses our relationships to perfect us through our love and care for one another.

The Bible clearly teaches us not to dismiss or avoid congregational worship in Hebrews 10:24-25; *And let us consider how we may spur one another on toward love and good deeds, not giving up meeting together, as some are in the habit of doing, but encouraging one another—and all the more as you see the Day approaching.* I suspect that Paul was referring to the church musicians when he said, "As some are in the habit of doing." While making music may bring you pleasure, purpose, and companionship with other musicians, you need more than your music to get through life. You need Godly companions that know the real you. Remember, even if you are employed in a different church, do all you can to maintain fellowship with your home church. Attend Bible studies when you can, show up for events, and let trusted fellow church members into your world. When the responsibilities of the music lifestyle complicate your life, these strong connections will help keep your mind and spirit healthy and your priorities focused.

Chapter Two

Stay Connected to your Spouse

"If I knew something useful to me and harmful to my family, I should put it out of my mind."

-Montesquieu

It's a feeling I never want to feel again. As I played another chorus of "Georgia On my Mind" or some other mournful song in a tiny blues hall, all I could think about was the phone call I'd have to make during the next break. I felt like a massive boulder was on top of me, pinning me to the keyboard bench.

My wife and I were seemingly at a dead-end in our marriage. While we'd survived transitions from my teaching career to full-time-ministry, and her transition from stay-at-home-mom to administrative manager in our church, it seemed our marriage was not going to survive our next transition. Somewhere between serving God and serving our kids, we forgot how to serve each other. In the meantime, we both made decisions that weakened our foundation as a couple.

I remember the empty expanse of dread and fear in my chest as I watched the audience swaying to the music with their drinks in hand. My chords were their soundtrack to fun and happiness – to me, they sounded like a funeral march. That audience had no idea that the guy supplying the lovely atmosphere for them was potentially saying goodbye to his marriage in a few minutes. The last thing I cared about at the time was the music.

Years later, thanks to God's immense grace, a lot of counseling, a million moments of forgiveness, and countless late nights talking and praying together, my wife and I's marriage is healthier and happier than it has ever been. But that night showed me that the love of an audience can't fill the space of an empty heart. If I can't connect emotionally with the person that I claim to love, it doesn't matter how many people are moved by my music.

The musical lifestyle can wreak havoc on a family unit of any type; married, with or without children, with siblings or extended family members. Every person connected to a musician can be affected. If we don't maintain healthy boundaries between our family responsibilities and our work, we risk losing the relationships that matter most. So we'll start with the most important relationship of all – the marriage relationship.

MUSIC AS A MISTRESS

Let's begin by acknowledging that marriage itself, or at least the act of remaining married for life, is becoming a lost art in our society. Divorce rates are rising, while cultural and social trends discourage people committing to one person for life. If you are a married musician, how can you maintain a healthy relationship when the music lifestyle demands so much time and effort away from the home and your spouse? And if you are not yet married, how can you manage the expectations your future spouse will have of you?

Jazz legend Duke Ellington's autobiography is entitled "Music is my Mistress". In it, he proudly states, "Music is my mistress, and she plays second fiddle to no one". Not surprisingly, Duke Ellington's romantic relationships were not ideal. His first marriage ended in separation, and his subsequent relationships were rocky and turbulent. Music, it seems, was not content to remain only a mistress. She wanted to have top priority.

CHEAT ON YOUR CAREER

Ellington's example is repeated often in the lives of misguided musicians who sabotage their marriage by having an affair with their career. A marriage should never play second fiddle to music. To ask your partner to do so is foolish and selfish. During a ministry workshop, I heard a pastor say that he has to choose to cheat on his ministry rather than cheat on his wife. Even though he is responsible for the spiritual growth of his church, his first priority is the health and growth of his marriage. Those who perform music for a living must make the same choice. If you aren't actively prioritizing your marriage, you are likely choosing your career over your commitment to your spouse.

I don't say these things to make you feel guilty or imply that every moment spent away from our spouses puts our marriages in danger. I simply want to reinforce the importance of *communication*. Many marriages are destroyed because neither spouse makes their expectations known. You may think you are on the same team, but can actually be following two different game plans. The old adage goes, "If you fail to plan, you plan to fail". This is certainly true for married musicians. We must plan to make our marriages work despite the unique demands of the musical lifestyle. Every decision should be made by husband and wife, working as a team, rather than two people headed toward different destinations.

Allen C. Paul

AUTHENTICITY

Knowing how to manage emotions is an important skill for a musician. Sometimes you don't feel like smiling and being happy on stage, but you overcome it because you know it's the right thing to do professionally. However, in your marriage, hiding your real feelings and putting on a show can be a death trap for your relationship.

Imagine spending an evening singing songs about freedom and love, only to return to a home where there is only disappointment and heaviness. Eventually, the mask falls off when an artist tries to pass off a persona that doesn't exist at home. My advice? Drop the act when it comes to your sharing your feelings with your spouse. If things aren't going right, say so. Communicating your true feelings is the only way to keep an authentic connection with your partner.

Married musicians also need to make sure to express the same passion and emotion at home that they express on stage. Husbands, don't let your wives see you handing out roses to the girls in the front row while you send her cheap Hallmark cards on Valentine's Day. Ladies, if you have to play the sexy siren act on stage, be just as willing to wow your husband at home. Your audience only gets a snapshot of your passion and personality. Your spouse should get the entire picture.

If your spouse is musically inclined, handling the pressures of the music lifestyle may seem like an easier task.

After all, you both know about the time and effort required to make it in music, right? As a pianist married to a vocalist, let me assure you that it isn't easier. In fact, when you are working in the same area, the temptation can be to form your entire relationship around your music. That doesn't work either. Inevitably, both of you need to break away from your work roles. Singing duets on stage doesn't always lead to sweet music behind closed doors. There has to be authenticity in your relationship, even if you are both performers, so that the love songs on stage don't turn into break-up songs backstage.

FAITHFULNESS AND FIDELITY

A lack of communication is not the only threat to a happy marriage. The industry is full of opportunities to be led astray, willingly or unwittingly, to disastrous decisions. Yes, I'm referring to infidelity and sexual temptation. Accountability, prayer, and self-discipline are keys to being strong in this area. I would go so far to say that if you are susceptible to sexual temptation, then you may want to reconsider music as a career. I don't mean to scare you if you are single, but I want you to be aware of the challenges you will face.

Besides the obvious temptations that come with late nights in clubs and tours far away from home, some temptations arise among our closest connections. We spend a lot of time with our bands, in studios and on tours, sometimes much more than we do with our families. Unfortunately, some marriages are broken up by illicit relationships between band members or other associates. For married musicians, extra care must be taken to keep our business relationships strictly professional.

There's no better way to emphasize the importance of guarding our fidelity than repeating Paul's warning in 1 Thessalonians 4:2-7 (NLT).

For you remember what we taught you by the authority of the Lord Jesus. God's will is for you to be holy, so stay away from all sexual sin. Then each of you will control his own body and live in holiness and honor-- not in lustful passion like the pagans who do not know God and his ways. Never harm or cheat a Christian brother in this matter by violating his wife, for the Lord avenges all such sins, as we have solemnly warned you before. God has called us to live holy lives, not impure lives.

There will always be challenges to our marriages, but we should never invite or encourage those threats by making unwise choices. When we allow sexual temptation to enter into our world, we're jeopardizing our Christian witness, our influence, and most of all, our vow of faithfulness to our spouses.

WHAT IF I'M NOT MARRIED?

I can't speak with authority on the life of a single musician, as I've been a married man for most of my adult life. I can tell you what my single friends in music have told me, and they all agree that dating is not easy these days. Many of them desire to be married one day, and they will have to prepare for the challenges we've already discussed. If you are single and thinking about getting married, you can use this book to your advantage. You've now seen the necessity of balancing music and marriage issues without having to experience them. You can avoid trouble spots before they happen in your relationship by focusing on trust and communication.

However, it's important to note that single musicians have to adjust quickly when they begin a long-term relationship. Many are used to taking gigs whenever they can, and it can be a rude awakening when your prospective mate is not on the same page. As one musician in a long-term relationship explained, keeping an open dialogue with his significant other was crucial. He makes sure she is aware of all the sacrifices that his career requires.

I realize some single musicians have no plans to get married, and others have dealt with the pain of a divorce. I'm not qualified to offer advice in these areas, but if you're dealing with difficulties living the single lifestyle, I would strongly encourage you to find Christian communities and resources that can help you navigate it better. If you think marriage is in your future, start prioritizing your choices with your future spouse in mind.

THE NEVER-ENDING REHEARSAL

As musicians, we're accustomed to working on our music until we get it right. For certain performances, that process may take a few days, weeks, or even months. I want you to see your marriage as a rehearsal that never truly ends. You and your spouse can continue to practice the skills of communication, trust, service, and honesty each and every day, and you can learn to love the process just as much as you enjoy learning new music. The duet you and your spouse can create may not always be in perfect harmony, but with God's help and your commitment, it can grow sweeter and sweeter with every passing day. Remember, making your marriage work will be one of the most important performances of your life. Choose to make it a priority.

> ### Conversations with the Pros: Camilo Velandia

Camilo Velandia has showcased his remarkable guitar skills on the world's biggest stages, having toured with Julio Iglesias, Jon Secada, and other internationally known artists. While handling his responsibilities on tour, he works hard to stay connected to his family back home. Camilo and his wife have been married for four years, and recently became parents with the arrival of their son, Logan. He talks about the challenges of being married while working as a touring musician.

Allen Paul: What's the greatest benefit of being a touring musician? And the greatest drawback?

Camilo Velandia: I think I can assume that most aspiring musicians for working musicians have always wanted to tour and play in large stadiums and arenas. I think it comes from the fact that in our culture, when a kid decides he wants to grow up to be a musician, nobody really takes them seriously. Kind of like the scenario where the girl introduces her musician boyfriend to her dad. Somehow, musicians are viewed as these lazy, drinking, smoking party animals. That changes the day you tour/perform/record with a major artist; NOW you're really something. I think part of our desire to tour and perform for thousands, is the desire to show everyone that what we work for year after year really pays off. The biggest drawback is trying to maintain some kind of normality with your life. People see touring musicians as these dudes that play packed venues and make lots of money, but they don't realize you spend a LOT of time in a plane, in an airport, in a bus, in a hotel lobby... Not to mention how hard touring can be for your personal relationships, just because you are not physically there.

AP: What is the biggest challenge of being married while on tour?

CV: I am blessed to have a wife that is very understanding. We love each other, and the hardest moment is always the day before I have to leave. I think the most important thing is to not get used to being without each other. We have to miss each other and really hurt so that when we see each other again it will all be worth it. The biggest challenge of being married while on tour is that within itself. Being away for long is very difficult, but the danger begins when you allow yourself to get used to being away, and talking less, and losing contact, because then, the relationship begins to fade.

AP: What strategies do you and your wife use to stay connected while you're apart?

CV: Thankfully, we live in a time where technology keeps us connected. I use that to my advantage. I have a cell phone plan where I have unlimited browsing and texting outside the country, so we text all day, and we skype/facetime throughout the day. We also send each other pictures and audio files of what we are doing throughout the day. In a way, it keeps us connected and informed of what the other one is doing.

AP: Did your spouse know the struggles and issues of being married to a musician before you got married?

CV: She had a good idea of what she was getting into. Nothing can really prepare you until it happens.

AP: What kind of situations have you faced on tour that made it tougher to be away from home?

CV: The first rough situation I went through was when I caught a fever with an ear infection in Brazil. Several other people got it too. Touring is very rough on your immune system if you aren't on top of it. I remember me in a bed, so sick I would constantly pass out. Luckily, we were off for almost a week, so the three roughest days I was able to be in bed, but the idea of being thousands of miles from home, with no one to really bring me some medicine or food, was pretty harsh. I was also fairly new to the tour, so I didn't know the guys well enough to ask for favors, etc.

AP: How do you handle situations when artists and tours require more time than you are willing to take away from home?

CV: It's always been a little different. The tours I have had thus far don't have runs that go longer than four weeks. My longest run was seven weeks, but then I get to come home and not work because I can get through with the money from the touring. However, this year I got an offer for a tour that was straight work from February 2015 to February 2016 with only five weeks off. I ended up turning it down because it felt like it was going to be too hard, and we had a baby on the way.

AP: How does your faith help you maintain a healthy marriage as a touring musician?

CV: I was one of two Christians in a group of almost 30 people, so I was always surrounded by drugs and alcohol. Lucky for me, I have never liked alcohol and never liked drugs. Not even from a faith point of view, but in general, I don't like it. One thing that I learned was that I had to be very humble about my beliefs. When people know you're a Christian, they tend to involve you less in hangs because they feel you're going to judge them and look down on them, so I never judged anyone for anything they did. Instead, I made sure that everyone knew that even if they were doing things that I don't do, I still love them and cherish their friendship on the road. That being said, you always gotta take care of yourself and keep margin lines, standards, and limitations. I made sure to never spend any time alone with anyone of the opposite sex, or to even have any intimate friendships. Keeping certain limitations helps you from feeding anything that will lead into something that could destroy your marriage. It's very important to keep the Word as your standard for everything, so that things don't slowly start to become acceptable.

Chapter Three

Stay Connected to your Children

"Behold, children are a gift of the LORD, The fruit of the womb is a reward."

-Psalms 127:3 NASB

My wife and I have three awesome kids. They are all young adults now, but they grew up as choir kids. In other words, they were always either in a choir rehearsal or waiting for one to end. We often joked that our second and third children were born singing three-part harmony because they heard it while in the womb so much. My oldest son was blessed with perfect pitch, which is both amazing and aggravating to his dad who did not receive the perfect pitch anointing. While all of my children have grown to love music and performing, we're not pushing them to become artists. We are proud of them because they are unique, special, loving individuals who have gifts and talents outside of music. We aren't a musical family only. We are a family first.

Having children is a life-changing experience that teaches life isn't about us, but about giving our children everything they need to become all God wants them to be. Parenting is a tremendous responsibility, no matter what your profession is, but musicians have unique challenges when we take on this role. We have to be 100% dedicated to our children, while simultaneously building a career that often requires irregular hours and unpredictable changes in lifestyle. How can we keep our children from being adversely affected as we pursue our dreams? Here are six key points:

1. Be a parent first.
2. Don't be too proud to change.
3. Build a support system.
4. Include the kids' input in goals and planning.
5. Don't try to force a love for music.
6. Spend time being a 'normal' family.

BE A PARENT FIRST, AN ARTIST SECOND

It's easy to see how the entertainment industry can destroy a family. Whether it's the Lohans, Kardashians, Biebers, or any other family that's constantly in the media, they almost inevitably end up in some type of crisis. One theme seems to apply to each of these reality show blow-ups. Somewhere along the line, image becomes more important than parenting. Money, fame, and celebrity get in the way of raising a child, and the results are plastered on social media and reality TV.

Children in musical families face similar dangers. The lifestyle of a musician, whether inside or outside of church, is largely based on a look-at-me mentality. Parents can become captive to living out their dreams while neglecting the dreams and needs of the children they brought into the world. I don't think any good parent deliberately sabotages the dreams of their children. However, in the midst of concerts, rehearsals, promotions, recordings, and the other activities of a music career, it is easy to be pulled away from the responsibilities of parenthood.

When I was a full-time minister of music, my children were often stuck at church waiting for me to finish a choir practice or musician rehearsal. Thankfully, our church was a comfortable place for them, but gradually they began to resent how much time ministry took from our family. More importantly, I neglected to schedule family outings where we could unplug, have fun and let the children be children. While I was dedicated to excellence in ministry, I was blind to the needs of my family.

One of my worst parenting moments occurred during a busy evening at my church. It was the weekend of Easter, and that Saturday evening, I was in the sanctuary long past midnight, preparing sound and other equipment for the set of services. I was stressed and sleepy, but I felt like I was doing the right thing by making sure every detail was ready. That's when I got a phone call from an unknown number. I answered, and my heart sank. It was a chaperone from my son's choir. They had completed a late performance, and he was the last child waiting at the theater. I had forgotten to pick him up.

The drive to that theater was filled with angry tears and guilt, knowing that I had lost sight of my first job – being a good father and keeping my kids first in my mind. Though my son probably barely remembers that late night waiting for his dad, I've never forgotten, because I never want to have that feeling again.

I don't mean to diminish the great privilege it is to work in music ministry while raising a family. Children do benefit from watching their parents work and serve in God's house faithfully and consistently. However, if ministry undermines our focus on nurturing our children's hearts and souls, our well-intentioned service to the church can become an idol that will harden the hearts of our kids. We must be parents first, and musicians and artists second. To our children, we're not recording artists or praise leaders. We are moms and dads. It's up to each musician to ensure that they never exchange the latter titles for the former ones.

Advice from the Pros

"There are many people – husbands, wives – that serve the house of God better than they serve their own house. Our first ministry is at home."

-Khristian Dentley (www.dentleyboyrecords.com)

DON'T BE TOO PROUD TO CHANGE

When our young children throw tantrums or beg for a toy for the thousandth time, we momentarily wish we could skip a few years of childhood and have our troubled toddlers go straight to graduation. That is, until they actually grow up. Then we wish they were small again and that we could relive those moments. Change is inevitable. As our children mature, they change and adjust to new seasons of their lives. Similarly, parents in the music field must be ready to make major changes in order to keep their families in working order. For some, that may mean an adjustment in the type of music career or goal you're pursuing. Sometimes, a dream for success has to be deferred for the sake of your children.

Maybe that big tour will have to wait till your child is old enough to travel. Perhaps the new home studio has to be converted into a nursery. It may be tough, but the sacrifice is worth it when you value your children's well-being over your career. Even if you are not currently connected with your children's other parent, plan your career around the needs of your children so that you can be present, involved, and active.

> ### Conversations with the Pros: Lavie and Stephane Murphy

Recording artist Lavie (www.lavie-music.com) and her husband Stephane Murphy are both professional musicians. Stephane began his training as a pianist, but after asking for a bass guitar as a gift, he quickly mastered the instrument and began touring with several reggae and gospel artists. Meanwhile, Lavie began her musical career as a backup singer for local artists in South Florida, while raising her daughter from a previous marriage. At the beginning of their marriage, they were often apart, as Stephane was on tour for months at a time. However, things changed when they discovered Lavie was pregnant with twins. In just a few months, she lost her job and was placed on bed rest. Stephane had to make a choice: stay on tour and support the family financially, or come home and physically become the anchor for his growing family.

He chose the latter – much to the surprise of his tour band mates and, perhaps more so, to his wife. Lavie admits that she resented his choice for a season, but they worked out their differences and are now raising their three children and promoting Lavie's solo career. Lavie says, "I know now there is purpose in our relationship." Stephane adds, "I have to love my wife as Christ loved the church. It's more important to be a family than an artist."

BUILD A SUPPORT SYSTEM

Despite all efforts to spend lots of quality time with your children, eventually a musical career requires time away from them. This is where a support system of childcare providers is so important. I am so thankful to the many babysitters, friends and family who provided a safe and fun place for my children when I went away to perform. I believe my children's formative years were richer because they shared time with these amazing people. A key to successful parenting is having friends and family that provide love, support and attention to your kids when you are not present. However, it's important to remember that caregivers are an extension of your parenting, not a replacement. There has to be a lot of communication between parents and caregivers to ensure that there is stability and continuity for the children in a musical family. Whether it's a child care facility, grandparent, family friend, or some other arrangement, it's the relationship between them, your child, and yourself that will make the system work so that you can continue to work effectively without worry.

If you are struggling to find alternative arrangements for your children, talk to other parents who work in the music business. See how they manage their responsibilities and keep their children happy and safe. Consider babysitting exchange nights with other couples so that each couple has the freedom to work an event or enjoy a date night. Networking among families in the music industry is a great way to solve problems that are common to all of us.

INCLUDE THE FAMILY'S INPUT IN GOALS AND PLANNING

Obviously a four-year-old is not interested in whether or not daddy is going to play with a top 40 band or whether mommy is releasing a new jazz album now or later. However, older children should be allowed to have input when music causes major shifts in your family life. Letting children voice their feelings in a safe environment is a great way to ensure that they feel comfortable and respected. They may not need to know all the details of a decision, but it's comforting to know mom or dad is not going to head off on a new tour without explaining how long it will be, how they will stay in touch, etc. In fact, by letting our children participate in our decisions as artists, we teach them about following their dreams and taking risks. That is an invaluable lesson that will help them in any field or profession they choose to pursue.

DON'T TRY TO FORCE A LOVE FOR MUSIC

Have you heard of helicopter parents? These are parents that hover over their children's every move, refuse to let their children operate independently, and vicariously live through their children's accomplishments. This suffocating environment can stifle children who are trying to become functioning, independent adults. When a parent can't let go at the appropriate time, it's hard for children to find their own paths.

Some parents behave in this way too. They assume that their children are born with talent and will share a love for music. It is true in many cases that the children of musical parents become musicians themselves, as they are exposed to the lifestyle and practice of music at an early age. However, this is not a given, and every parent in the music field should be careful not to assume their child will gravitate toward music. Your children are individuals with their own unique skills, likes, and abilities, so be careful not to make their career choices for them. Should they be exposed to music? Yes! Should they be expected to choose music as a career? Absolutely not. Let them see the enjoyment you get from your craft, and if they ask to become more engaged in it, by all means encourage them. Never assume music is the family business. God might be leading your children in a different direction.

SPEND TIME AS A NORMAL FAMILY

Both the worlds of ministry and music can be very isolated from other professions, and the circles that your family will engage with may be small at times. This is why you should make it a priority to expose your children to a wide variety of activities. Not every social event has to be church or music related. Make sure to schedule time off to vacation. Take your children on boy's nights out or daughter-dates where you can spend time one-on-one. Leave the cell phone off when you attend their events. Don't let the fast-paced lifestyle of church, gigs, and rehearsals take over your family. You only have your children in your care for a short time. Cherish them more than you cherish your career.

ALLEN C. PAUL

Conversations With The Pros: Khristian Dentley

In a few short months, Khristian Dentley was elevated from a local church worship leader to a member of the iconic gospel/jazz vocal ensemble TAKE 6. When he was first asked to join the group, he felt that God had provided an amazing blessing in his life and career. However, he notes that after joining the ensemble, he lost the balance between music and family for a season. He would come back from tour and immediately become immersed in work again, which took a toll on his relationships. Khristian uses a musical analogy to illustrate how he had to address the situation. He says musicians are very accustomed to the term 'balance' when it comes to hearing parts of their music played. A good producer listens back to a recording over and over in order to ensure that the right parts are heard clearly. In the same way, a musician must be able to monitor the balance of his family. When one track, time with family, is not being accented enough, a musician has to turn up the volume of family time and turn down the noise of a career. This principle applies even when the musician works in a church. Khristian states emphatically, "There are many people – husbands, wives –

that serve the house of God better than they serve their own house. Our first ministry is at home."

Taking all of this into account, balancing a music career and family life can be boiled down to one question: *How will this (gig, performance or opportunity) affect my family?* Do you ask yourself that question when you are asked to perform, travel, or spend time away from home? If not, you to start doing that. Every time you're asked. No exceptions.

If you answer that question honestly each time, you can avoid the consequences of over-commitment. Should you take that Saturday night party gig if your spouse needs your help early in the morning to get the kids ready for church? Should you be taking on an extra rehearsal when the kids don't see you until almost bedtime three or four nights a week? Never forget that short-term financial benefits aren't worth doing long-term damage to your family relationships.

If you are trying to make a living with your music, don't forget that you have to make a life for your family as well. It's a hard pill to swallow, but every musician must decide if a full time music career will provide adequate income for their family. If not, you might have to make some tough choices regarding your career. This doesn't mean you should give up on your dreams of playing music professionally. It means that your family's needs must take top priority. Moving ahead with your career without considering the sacrifices your family must make will create isolation. This isolation will lead to a loss of perspective. You can always write another song or play another gig. You can't replace time with your loved ones.

In conclusion, remember the way Jesus emphasized the danger of prioritizing success over relationships: *What good is it for someone to gain the whole world, and yet lose or forfeit their very self?* (Luke 9:25) Jesus was speaking of giving up the promise of eternal life for the temporary joys of worldly success. But the same analogy works when it comes to your family and your career as well. Your family is an extension of you. The world of music may promise fame, respect and validation, but true success is found when your family is happy, healthy and whole. Put them first.

Chapter Four

Stay Connected to God

"The most important thing I get from my relationship with the Creator is simply that the music doesn't come from me."

-Marcus Miller

At first glance, staying connected to God may seem too obvious to be addressed. Surely you are maintaining a connection to God. After all, you're reading a book with God in the title. Let's do a simple test. Get a pen and paper and answer the following questions:

1. Do I consistently study the Bible?
2. Do I have set devotional times and keep them?
3. Do I pray regularly when things *aren't* going wrong?

Don't feel guilty if you answer no to all three questions, but recognize that answering in that manner raises a red flag about your relationship with God.

If you play regularly for worship services, you may feel that your service in church equals your God connection. Wrong! A musician can play music for God's people, in God's house while not being a part of God's family. Unfortunately, many musicians cover up a lack of spiritual commitment with a mask of talent and ability. Even the best, most skillful Christian musicians and artists can find themselves lost without a foundation of faith that is only built on the daily practice of walking with God. Spiritual apathy will always occur when your relationship with God is not your top priority.

Perhaps you've never considered that your interests can interfere with your spiritual health, but they can. If we're not careful, our love of music may develop into an idol just as destructive as lust, pride, or any other sin. You cannot keep your artistic life in its proper perspective without strong faith and a connection to Jesus Christ. Without his guidance, our creative abilities can become a burden rather than a blessing to ourselves and to others.

Christian musicians can stay plugged in to God by employing the same spiritual tools that are given to every believer: prayer and reading God's word. There are specific ways that you can apply these disciplines to your career.

PRAYER

If you only pray once in a while, you are missing out on the power of this spiritual discipline. James 5:16 reminds us that the *prayers* (plural) of the righteous are effective. If we have lazy and inconsistent prayer habits, we can be sure that our prayers are not reaching the level of effectiveness that can change our lives. Here are some simple steps, all related to the music profession, that will help you develop a stronger daily prayer habit.

PRAY BEFORE YOU PERFORM

This step may seem awkward for those of us who play songs at gigs with very little, if any, positive spiritual content. Some may assume that God has no interest in blessing our performances that include non-Christian messages. Let's examine the response of a man in the Bible who also had to serve in a place where God was not being worshipped.

In the fifth chapter of 2 Kings, we are introduced to Naaman, a Syrian captain, who is suffering from leprosy. His king encourages him to seek healing from Elisha, who was Israel's prophet at the time. Namaan doesn't initially believe in the God Elisha serves nor the method that Elisha uses to cure him, but he eventually gives in to Elisha's instructions and is healed. This healing opens his eyes to the truth of God's authority, and he accepts Jehovah as the one true God. Now cured of his leprosy, he then must return to his country to serve his king. Before he returns, Naaman makes this request of Elisha in verse 18. *However, may the LORD pardon me in this one thing: When my master the king goes into the temple of the god Rimmon to worship there and leans on my arm, may the LORD pardon me when I bow, too.* (2 Kings 5:18 NLT) Naaman clearly recognized that his master was serving a false god, but he had to go back to his job in a place that did not share his new beliefs. He prayed that God would forgive him as he continued his vocation in a pagan land.

Naaman is not the only servant in the Bible that worked among those that practiced the exact opposite of his faith. Joseph and Moses both served in the Egyptian government. Daniel, Shadrach, Meshach, and Abednego all worked for the Babylonians. Nehemiah was a cup-holder in the Babylonian palace. Did any of these faith-filled men abandon their posts because the environment was hostile to their faith? No.

Instead, they stayed and used their Godly influence to impact the rulers and leaders that they served. Each of them used prayer as a foundation while they served in positions that were seemingly incompatible with their beliefs.

In the same way, we often work in places where the music conflicts with our convictions. These are challenging environments, but God can use us in these places to reach people who otherwise may never step into a church or consider accepting Christ. This is why you must pray before every performance. Ask God to reinforce your inner convictions when the music you perform, for whatever reason, doesn't square with your beliefs. Like Naaman, you may have to support your employer, but your true King is on the throne in your heart. While we cannot control every action or thought that surrounds our profession, we do control our motives and attitude toward our Father as we perform.

PRAY BEFORE YOU PRACTICE

Serious musicians know that we only master our instruments through consistent practice. We rehearse, review songs, and spend countless hours on our instruments to perfect our abilities. How can we improve our mental focus as we hone our skills? Simply by asking God to bless and direct our practice time.

Praying for God's discipline and wisdom each time you sit down to rehearse will do wonders for your mental state and, more importantly, your ability to sense God's direction in your creative decisions. "Every good and perfect gift is from above" says James 1:17. If we are to honor God with our gift, we must pray for his guidance when we prepare to use it.

A key component of prayer is intention. When you sit down to practice, ask God to reveal the weak areas in your techniques or in your abilities. My favorite practice saying is "Sit down, find something you can't play, and don't get up 'til you can play it." Without clear intention, we sometimes don't know what to practice first. I believe prayer can unlock creative understanding so we can know exactly what will improve our gift and how to approach each practice session.

When God gave instructions on the construction of the tabernacle, and later the temple, he also gave his workmen and musicians special insight and skills that would enable them to complete the work. God did not do the work for them. Prayer before a rehearsal doesn't replace effort, discipline, and professionalism. Instead, prayer should reinforce your commitment to do everything with excellence. God can infuse your practice time with the divine wisdom and skill you will need to accomplish everything he wants you to achieve with your talent.

PRAY BEFORE YOUR DAY

Every Christian needs to connect with God on a daily basis, but musicians and artists need consistent prayer time in a special way. Musicians need constant communication with the Lord to balance our creative and spiritual lives. It is very easy for musicians to blame their irregular schedules and late hours for an inability to maintain a regular and consistent prayer life. That excuse doesn't hold up. The same discipline that it takes to work on your gift is the same discipline it takes to keep your prayer time. No particular place or time is more holy than another. It is the act of prioritizing a specific place and time that honors God.

When we pray daily, we should remember that God desires a two-way communication with us. His Word tells us that he knows all that we need before we ask, and this would include our desire to create music and to be successful. According to Matthew 6:33, our first request of God should be to seek his righteousness. When we adopt his will as our own, he then ensures that we will receive everything we need to succeed in life.

Psalms 37:4 states, "Take delight in the LORD, and he will give you the desires of your heart.." Every artist wants to make an impact on the world. There is nothing wrong with that God-given desire. However, our prayer time should rekindle and refocus our delight in the Lord, so that our desire for success never distracts us from the true source of our life and strength. Daily prayer for God's will and rule in our lives keeps our drive to succeed in the proper perspective.

To build support in your prayer life, consider joining a prayer group within your ministry or with a local circle of musicians. Several ministries have created networks and prayer groups that encourage spiritual growth and encouragement. One of these groups is Aaron Lindsey's 414 Ministries. Aaron is a multi-Grammy award winning producer who has been a part of some of the most successful gospel music releases in history, working with artists such as Israel Houghton and Marvin Sapp. Not content with musical success alone, he created a ministry that reached out to musicians and creative artists via a weekly prayer call. When we join with other artists to make prayer a priority, we strengthen the entire Christian community.

READING THE BIBLE

The Bible is widely acknowledged as the world's bestselling book. However, it may be the only book on the best seller list that is not consistently read by those who claim to respect and revere its teachings. There is more access to God's Word today than at any time in history, but few Christians study the Bible regularly. Unfortunately, this form of biblical illiteracy is shared by some musicians that play every Sunday.

You don't have to look hard to see the results of this lackadaisical approach to the Bible. Find a musician who doesn't prioritize learning and practicing the principles of God's Word, and you're also likely to find a musician with confused beliefs, lack of faith, weak convictions and no passion for the local church. In contrast, those musicians who maintain a consistent Bible study time are more stable, grounded, and capable of handling any circumstance they face.

The Bible itself explains how it should guide our decisions in everyday life; *all scripture is inspired by God and is useful to teach us what is true and to make us realize what is wrong in our lives. It corrects us when we are wrong and teaches us to do what is right.* (2 Timothy 3:16 NLT)

It is impossible for you to sustain your faith on and off the stage without a dedication to daily Bible reading and application. All of the spiritual and emotional issues we face in our lives and careers are addressed there. It is imperative that we open our hearts and minds to what God says to us in his book. There are three strategies that will help you build and strengthen your Bible reading discipline: doing word studies, using technology, and joining a small bible study group.

4. Do a word study on music in the Bible

This method of studying the Bible involves finding every mention of a certain word and making note of the meaning, context, and applications found when it appears. Since music is our profession, it makes sense to discover all we can about music in the Bible. To do a word study, you will need a study Bible, a web-based or printed concordance (a list of all words that appear in the Bible), and a dictionary for comparison to modern terms. Take one verse or passage per week and study how music was applied in Biblical times. Make note of how important music was in various situations, from prophetic moments to times of praise. Pick a verse that epitomizes your career and memorize it.

As you read and study, don't forget to live out what you read. Sing like David sang when you are in trouble or hurting. Pray like Daniel when you are faced with opposition. The Word only has power in your life when you act on it.

USE TECHNOLOGY FOR CONSTANT ACCESS

In this day of smart phones, social media, and instant communication, we are blessed to have access to the Bible in any form, anywhere. We can download and view the Bible in every translation and access it in audio or visual form. But still many of us find ourselves not making use of this gift of technology. To remedy this, consider an online reading plan that will take you through the entire Bible in a year, or some other form of daily reading plan from apps such as YouVersion, Bible Gateway, Olive Tree, and Blue Letter Bible. Having reminders from these sites will help you to maintain your Bible reading in the midst of gigs and rehearsals.

When I had an hour-long commute to a music class every week, I used the audio feature of my Bible app to listen to my Bible in the car. I found I could easily finish ten chapters during my drive. Using technology as a tool to assist my daily Bible reading proved to be a valuable part of maintaining my discipline.

GET INVOLVED WITH A BIBLE STUDY

There is nothing that can replace the connection that a small group study can provide when looking into the Bible. When combined with personal Bible study, the input and encouragement of other believers who are opening their hearts to the same scriptures increases the effectiveness of what we've learned. Many churches have weekly bible studies or small group studies on various topics of the Bible. Rather than avoiding these studies due to your busy schedule, make it a point to be there. The support, understanding, and accountability you will receive as you prioritize the study of God's Word is much more valuable than a night off or a gig opportunity. If your church does not provide weekly Bible study, considering hosting one in your home. Even better, invite your friends to join you. You'd be surprised at how many musicians are looking for a place to help them better understand the Word.

BEING A LIGHT IN DARK PLACES

As believing musicians, we often will work and perform in places where the Christian culture is not welcome, or at least not celebrated. It may be that you are blessed to work with many Christian musicians; perhaps you are the only professing Christian in your band or on your gig. As I said earlier, staying connected to God does not mean we should abandon every job or gig that does not have Christian influences. Christians are called to be "a city set on a hill" in Matthew 5:14. We are commanded to represent the light of God's love in all situations while always giving him the credit for our talent.

Jesus represents this balancing act best. The Pharisees constantly accused him of being a sinner because he hung out with the wrong crowd. For example, think of his presence at the wedding celebration of Cana. This celebration was likely full of the same things we find in today's wedding receptions:

music, partying, and yes, drinking! Jesus, however, was not there simply to celebrate. He placed himself in a position to meet a need that no one else could meet. In the same way, God will give you opportunities to represent Christ to your peers, but only if you are willing to stay connected to the compass of his direction.

The Christian's struggle to be in the world but not of the world is not new. Paul wrote extensively in his letters to believers who wavered over which practices of the world to reject. Likewise, we must be careful about how we are presenting ourselves. Ask yourself questions that can help you check your position. Am I consistent in my walk and talk? Am I both humble and transparent? Do I uphold my own moral standards? Do I waver when I'm tempted to join in questionable behavior? This fine line between 'in the world' and 'of the world' requires us to access God's wisdom, spirit, and direction at all times. What may be acceptable behavior in one situation may not be okay in another. Rather than making a list of things to do and not do, I urge you to consistently pray for discernment. James 1:5 tells us that God will give wisdom to anyone who asks him in sincerity. If we want the right answers, we must ask the right person: the Holy Spirit.

Before finishing the discussion about connections, some hard questions need to be asked.

- What would you do if you were unable to play music?
- Can you imagine a life where you had no musical skill?
- Now ask yourself, would you still worship God without that skill available?

If you can't say yes, then you need to look beyond your music and deepen your relationship with the God who gave you your talent in the first place.

If you don't have a praise and worship life outside of your music, and you look forward to the crowds at your gigs more than the time of devotion and study of the Bible, you are in serious danger of losing the one connection that matters most. Your creativity, passion, and sensitivity all stem from the inner peace and strength that your walk with God provides. When you are in tune spiritually, you'll be much more in tune musically.

Advice from the Pros

Every door that opens, every great relationship, every stage is designed to give you the influence and draw certain people to you, so that what you have to say off stage will affect their life in a positive way! If we always look at the "secular" opportunities through these eyes, we'll keep in perspective the types of gigs we search for and accept. Consider the amount and level of spiritual testing and compromise you'd have to deal with on a consistent basis! Is it really worth your soul? My advice is to be wise and always allow GOD to order your steps!

- Trent Phillips

Remember to uphold your standards and convictions. It's hard to minister on a Sunday if the worshipers of your congregation see you in deep sin on a Friday or Saturday.

- Victor Russo, bassist and engineer
(www.inthemixaudio.com)

ALLEN C. PAUL

God can get glory out of anything and anyone, but let's be musicians that make him our first priority and seek his desires first. Everything else we are destined to receive will arrive in his perfect timing.

Part II: Your Career

CHAPTER FIVE

Establish your Priorities

Things which matter most must never be at the mercy of things which matter least.

– Goethe

Perhaps it was when I was allowed backstage in a dressing room with Gladys Knight and Whoopi Goldberg walked in that it hit me. *This* was the big time. I had just finished the biggest gig of my life up to that point, playing an opening set with my best friend, singer and songwriter Neville Peter, for a concert featuring Gladys in Toronto. Since I was still a college student, I was both exhilarated and intimidated by the task of being the musical director for Neville's band. I was grateful that the studio musicians, all much more experienced, were friendly and great to work with. After the set, I was approached by the director for Gladys' band, who gave me his card and told me to call him anytime. Certainly this was my big break!

However, once I returned home, I made a decision, or more accurately, I decided *not* to do something. I never made the call. While I'm sure there would have been no harm in calling and maintaining contact, I was settled in my decision that my growing relationship with my soon-to-be-wife and my job prospects at home would be my focus. Through the years, I've been tempted to think about the could-have-beens, but I can always point to the things I may have missed out on. If I had chosen to jump into a world I was not ready for, I may have negatively influenced my future relationship with my wife, as well as many other relationships that developed soon after that opportunity. I was sure of my highest priorities and I was confident in making a decision that reflected them.

Working as a musician takes a level of commitment and decisiveness. You wouldn't have chosen this career if you did not have vision and determination. However, each day and moment of a musician's life requires us to make choices based on priorities we set long before the big breaks come our way.

First, we need to expand on the concept of priorities. It's not simply choosing to work at a church or going on a tour. Our priorities determine the outcome each life decision we make, and then filter down to our career decisions. You may make all of your income from playing for performance, including touring and traveling. This means you must set different priorities than a musician that has a full time job in another field. Perhaps you're heavily involved in studio recording and production, which keeps you mostly in town, but requires availability at odd hours. That type of lifestyle will require a different set of priorities professionally. Wherever your priorities lie, your choices will follow.

BE SURE OF YOUR IDENTITY

Before you decide what you will do, it's important to know *who you are.* I've met many musicians who wrap themselves in their musical identity. They are *what they do.* That is a dangerous way to define yourself. It takes more than a bunch of music awards and album credits to be successful as a musician. If we only desire the fame, glory, and rewards of the lifestyle, we may find ourselves unfulfilled even after we reach our goals.

My friend and band mate Alton is a musician who keeps his identity in perspective. He has been a drummer at my church for over 15 years. His job requires him to work overnight shifts several times a week. Even though a schedule change forced him to begin missing weekly rehearsals, he still comes to church every Sunday, sometimes straight from work, and is always prepared to play due to his discipline and preparation. Clearly, Alton has his priorities in order so that he can be faithful in everything he does, whether it be his career or his church position. When I asked him about how he does it, he commented, "Music is what I do; *it's not who I am.*"

Jesus said, "Where your treasure is, there your heart will be also" (Matt 6:21). Our treasure doesn't follow our heart; our heart follows our treasure. When we prioritize our time, our talent, and our resources in a place, our passions will grow in that direction. The key, then, is to determine our treasured places, musically, emotionally, and relationally. Those treasured places will then determine our priorities.

LOOK BACK AT YOUR MEMORIES

What has brought you the most joy since you became interested in music? Was it a memory from a certain teacher, a church service, a concert? Maybe from writing your first song? Connecting to your treasured memories can clue you in to your deepest passions. Maybe a combination of memories inspire you, but there are usually one or two areas where you feel most comfortable. That is where you can bet your musical heart is, and that will help you establish your priorities.

My favorite personal memories come from my childhood, with my family sitting around the piano. My mother was my first piano teacher, and my family and I spent many holidays and family gatherings singing while she or I accompanied them. To this day, those are some of my most treasured memories. It's not surprising then, that while I love composing, writing, and arranging, my greatest joy is performing with small groups of friends or music lovers as we enjoy each other's company. My passions all relate to connecting people through music. I can honestly say no other musical endeavor excites me more than that.

MOTIVATION

What makes you want to be a musician? What inspires you to work long hours and to sacrifice time and money to be successful? What are the driving forces that make you want to perform? There are three factors I think every working Christian musician can agree on.

To make great music: This is the most obvious motivation, but also the hardest one. We all desire to make timeless, creative, and unique music. However, it is likely that many of our creations will never reach the masses or become classics. The motivation to create great music has to be strong enough to outlast the frustration of the process and the possibility of anonymity.

To make a living: Despite the financial struggles many musicians face, the ability to earn a living is a key factor in choosing this career. Being a musician may never make you as rich as Warren Buffett or Bill Gates, but the desire to be compensated well for your work is nothing to be ashamed of.

To serve God: No matter where you perform, you can be motivated by the desire to serve God with your music. God gave you your talent, and when you share it you are serving and honoring him. The key to this motivation is connecting with the desires of God, so that your music goes *where he wants it to go*. When your passion is to please him, staying motivated is much easier. As Isaiah 40:28-31 states, those who place their hope in God will renew their strength even when others with more resources or talents stumble and fall.

Our motives determine what and where we perform. There will always be a need for musicians in the local church, and if you are called to music ministry, you should honor that calling. However, you can serve God while creating music in any style or genre. God doesn't limit his blessings to the inside of the church, and as Christian musicians, we should not let our motivation to produce excellent music be limited either.

3 LEVELS OF MUSICIANSHIP

You may not have to struggle with motivation or passion, but you may be struggling with your current level of accomplishment in the music industry. You can't move forward in your career unless you honestly assess where you are right now. In general, every musician falls into one of these categories:

- ⭕ Amateur
- ⭕ Semi-pro
- ⭕ Professional

Amateur – If you are an amateur, you enjoy playing or singing, but you have little to no desire to become a performing artist. You might be content to minister in the local church, for friends and loved ones, and perhaps you have enough skill to perform for fun within the local scene. However, you don't have the passion or the time to become a full-time working musician. I included this category because without amateurs, many churches would cease to have effective music ministries. We all want high quality, professional level music in our worship services, but that is impossible when you consider the number of churches compared to the pool of professionally trained musicians. Amateurs may have a high level of talent, but the key difference is that they have no desire to make music their full-time vocation. Many volunteer choir and praise ensemble members fit into the amateur category.

Semi-pro – As a semi-pro, you have a higher level of musical skill, some formal training, and you may perform occasionally in the local scene or worship services. The difference between the amateur and the semi-pro is that you've has made music part of their career path. You may have a full-time job but also perform on weekends, write songs, or dream of recording an album someday. Perhaps you're waiting for an opportunity to become professional, but you haven't had the break you are looking for. However, if you are a semi-pro, you should be honest with yourself about the steps you need to take to become a professional. If your passion and motivation is only for financial success or fame, you are in for a rude awakening once you enter the professional ranks of musicians. You will have to make some sacrifices before you can consider yourself a professional. The best example of a semi-pro is a local musician or singer that frequents open mic events and performs on occasion, but for whatever reason, has not taken their career to the next level.

Professional – As a professional, you have dedicated your life to music. You might have another job, but the majority of your goals are directed toward your musical career. You may be a studio musician, a musical director, or perhaps an educator. When you're hired, people expect you a top-quality performance. You are determined to make an impact with your music and you're probably very entrepreneurial in spirit. Although being paid a professional rate helps to qualify your status, you aren't really a professional until the music community treats you like one. If your work is consistently on the same level as other pros in your field, professional respect will follow. Keep in mind that working in a ministry as a volunteer doesn't necessarily mean you don't perform at a professional level. It simply means you've chosen not to pursue compensation in that area. However, the norm is for professionals to be paid commensurate to their status.

If you are paid to play or perform in any type of gig or venue, you are probably in the professional category. Even though you have reached this level of musicianship, continue to re-evaluate your passions and desires periodically to see if you are consistently growing as a musician and artist. Remember; it's a bad idea to base your identity on what you currently are – even if you are very good at it.

CHOOSING A PATH

No matter what stage of musicianship you are in, eventually you have to decide what you will do with your talent. It is one thing to be blessed with an ability to sing or play an instrument, but sharing it effectively and consistently requires another level of commitment. Every musician must decide at some point to focus on a certain area of the profession. This path can change drastically over the course of a career, but it is always based on the proper analysis of your ability and the opportunities available, along with the passion and discipline you will need in order to be successful.

In his book "The Savvy Musician", David Cutler lists several areas in which musicians can earn income. Rather than labeling them as skills or disciplines, he names them 'products', because every musician must offer something tangible for an audience to purchase or support. His list includes Composition, Concertizing Ensembles, Gigging Ensembles, Music Lessons, Performances, Projects, Recordings, Recording Studios, and finally Marketing Yourself.[2] Each of these categories requires different choices and various types of preparation. Within each area, there are endless possibilities and opportunities you to explore. Choosing the right path requires a lot of discipline and understanding of your own goals and abilities.

Before you step into any project or career path, evaluate it carefully. Every opportunity is not necessarily the right one for you, even if it is lucrative, amazing, or seemingly a one-in-a-lifetime opening. Christians often refer to these opportunities as open doors. An illustration about doors that Amie Dockery of Covenant Church in Dallas, Texas, once preached about stuck with me. She explained that many of us see open doors as God's approval of an opportunity. But when a thief is searching a neighborhood for targets, they also look for open doors. It's as if we think the easiest path is always the right one, while God would have us ask, seek, and knock where the doors are not wide open. Once again, the key is found in prayer. We must always check with God in order to discern which opportunities he wants us to accept.

---

[2] "The Savvy Musician", David Cutler, pg.31-32

ALLEN C. PAUL

Conversations with the Pros

Born in Connecticut and raised in South Florida, Dwayne Bennett (www.saintorbin.com) has become a much sought after touring musician. He's a producer, bassist, guitarist, and keyboardist. He also anchors his church band as musical director.

Allen Paul: How do you respond to Christians that question the music you play professionally?

Dwayne Bennett: The church frowns on it [working in the popular music industry]. The world is a secular world. We're just not supposed to be of it. You're not worshipping when you are playing in a secular market. We have sacred moments in a secular world. Work is secular, worship is sacred. So if you are working at Publix, you're in a secular market. If you're playing for Beyonce, you're in a secular market, but you're not worshipping.

AP: How do you maintain your faith while on tour?

DB: I can truly say that world [touring] isn't for everybody. At the end of the day, you have to have a backbone and say, "I know who I belong to, whose child I am." I've seen people go into the touring world and leave the church. It has to do with who's feeding you at home, when you're not on the road. When I started touring, I was being taken care of at home, but this was an opportunity I knew I needed to step into. They [musicians that leave the church] go out because they aren't being taken care of. It's an escape, instead of an opportunity.

AP: How do you maintain your focus on ministry as a music professional?

DB: The way I was raised, ministry is always a priority. For instance, it's hard for me to say what's going on in church isn't important, because that's my life…because ministry is in me.

AP: Did you ever feel insecure about becoming a touring musician?

DB: I honestly felt like I could have been doing it [touring] earlier, and should have been doing it earlier, but I think there was an inner fear that was causing me not to move forward. The thing everybody used to say to me was, "I never thought you'd be interested in doing it." I was always down to tour, but I never put myself out there to do it. It was the uncertainty of knowing what it all entailed. 'If I'm going to be gone a long time, is this going to be able to pay my bills?' While you're thinking of all those things, you're not moving forward.

AP: How do you view the difference between working in music ministry versus working on tour?

DB: I don't appreciate when people treat the church as a job. You can't treat ministry like it's just a nine to five. On tour, you can treat it like a nine to five, because it's work. There's no spiritual attachment to that. You don't owe anybody anything like you owe God your service. When you go to church, you might get a check, but you're not going for a check, you're going to give God your best. You can't treat them [church and touring] the same at all.

DECIDE WHAT MATTERS

Setting priorities doesn't mean that every career decision will be easy. Conflicts in the musical lifestyle are unavoidable. There will be times when your church holds a special service at the same time that a major gig is available, or when a tour conflicts with an important family event. The pressure to choose correctly can become overwhelming for the performance minded musician, when in fact the choice should be made long before the conflict arises. If you have clearly defined the priorities of church work and being a responsible and dependable gigging musician, you can determine which gigs to take and which to decline.

Personally, I've chosen to place a high priority on being in attendance at my place of worship. There are other dedicated musicians who play with high-profile acts that have to travel frequently. While touring is certainly a worthwhile and exciting career path, at this point in my career, I've found that other priorities weigh more heavily. As a result, I've turned down offers to travel with other artists. This doesn't mean that those musicians who stay home are more faithful than those that travel. Worship and secular artists alike need qualified musicians with flexible schedules who can support tours and other out-of-town performances. However, even touring musicians must set priorities, especially when deciding how much time away is too much. If you don't set these limits before you begin traveling, you can find yourself in awkward or difficult circumstances. The best defense against misunderstandings is to communicate your priorities to all of your employers before you take a job or assignment.

Family priorities have already been discussed, but career priorities are also very important. Some musicians don't know what field of music they should specialize in. Being a jack of all trades may make you feel useful in several areas, but eventually, you will find that a lack of one priority translates to a lack of effectiveness in others. If you have strong skills in production and studio work, then you should be working a lot in that field. Those musicians that excel at accompanying and leading bands should be active in the live performance scene. Focus on what you do best.

The Bible clearly states that we are to count the cost before we build anything, including a career (Luke 14:28). By establishing your priorities, you can determine what costs you are willing to pay and which ones are too expensive financially, relationally, and spiritually. Plan wisely and you'll be better off in the long run.

> ## Conversations With The Pros: Parris Bowens

Born in Philadelphia, Pennsylvania, and raised playing in church, Parris Bowens is a keyboardist, songwriter, and producer. He was discovered by Tye Tribett and became a key member of Tribbett's band, Soundcheck. Parris co-wrote some of Tye's hit songs, such as No Way, Mighty Long Way and Hold On. He has worked with Musiq Soulchild, Timbaland, Brandy, Floetry, Gerald Levert, Vivian Green, Marvin Sapp, Kierra Sheard, Myron Butler, Kim Burrell, The Roots, Israel & New Breed and many other artists. At the time of this writing, he was working on his official release, "Theme of Dreams", with his brand Parris & The Revival. He is married to his wife, Dionne, and they have two boys.

Allen Paul: Tell us a little about how you got your start in music. What made you want to be a professional musician?

Parris Bowens: Well, I got my start in music because I

grew [up] in a musical family. [My] Dad is a pastor and [my] mom [is] a singing evangelist. One day, my Dad sat me down and taught me how to play because he needed someone at the church. I was about 10 or 11.

AP: What was the biggest struggle of your early career?

PB: FEAR. FEAR. FEAR. Early on in my life, I went through some traumatic things that led to a bit of people anxiety. So the irony of being on stage was that I had to face people. So when I started playing with an artist as exciting and radical as a Tye Tribbett, it took a while for me to adjust to the attention. I would try to hide out behind the curtain with my keyboard on stage. Or, I would keep my volume levels very low, and Tye would come back to the keyboard and turn my volume up. For a longtime, I didn't feel adequate. I had to break the cycle of fear.

AP: What relationships helped you develop as a young musician? Are those relationships still intact?

PB: Man, first my father. We were very close. I was his shadow. He instilled not only music, but also the intangibles like humility, order, professionalism, etc. After that, my first mentor was a local artist, John Payton. He heard [me] while I was backing my mother and invited [me] to play for his choir. He taught me about Jazz. He let me hangout with him at University of the Arts (in Philly) sometimes. That was an invaluable tool. And it was with him that Tye Tribbett discovered me. And with Tye (I consider that college years), I not only grew in music, but he discipled me and, through his ministry, I was truly saved. Another major mentor and contributor to my career was with James Poyser. He met me when I was about 15/16. And he was one of those guys that allowed [me] into their space and [showed] me the ropes in the studio. He actually was one of the few that started showing me how to read music. He's one of those life-long brothers. And I still have a relationship with every one of them to this day.

AP: How did you handle the transition to playing on tours? Did you play for your local church while traveling?

PB: Well, [as] soon as I got out of high school, I worked maybe two jobs over the course of a year, and in that time I connected with Tye. As soon as I connected with him, I was on a roller coaster ride. We gigged a lot up and down the East Coast. In some cases, that's not considered touring, but it was a setup, and with Tye, I immediately got a lot of exposure and validation. Anybody who plays with Tye can tell you he vets great musicians. From him, I connected with the whole Philly scene, both gospel and secular. So my first R & B gig was Eric Roberson, and it took a while for me to adjust because I grew up in a house that didn't listen to secular music. So I struggled back and forth, playing songs that didn't sound like home. Major culture shock. So there were gigs that I started rehearsals for, and then would quit before we hit the road. Lol. I know I made people mad. Just pure conviction. Then, ironically, I was prophesied to and told to take this gig with Floetry, and sure 'nough we won souls on that tour. At that time, me and Thaddeus Tribbett and George "Spanky" McGurdy was in the band. We'd go to the back of the bus after every show and turn on Cece Winans' Throne Room record. That would refresh and bring us back to a place we missed. That helped me handle the road. Accountability.

AP: Were there any moments that made you question your calling or ability to succeed as a musician? How did you respond?

PB: Absolutely. Again it was FEAR. I'll never forget early on with Tye, I told him that was afraid of being on stage, and he said to me, "Then quit! There's a whole line of other guys waiting for the opportunity if you don't want it." And I know that he wasn't saying that to be mean. He said it to challenge me and to really look at what FEAR was gonna rob me of. I immediately gathered my thoughts and spoke to myself. And I still fought FEAR every gig after that, but I faced it head on until, one day, I became free, and then I actually started playing too loud!

AP: How do you maintain your personal walk with God while working in high level, high pressure musical environments?

PB: I always tell people that some of the most powerful experiences I've had with God have been outside the four walls of the church. When I was seeking God for a baptism of the Holy Spirit, I was at every altar call praying, tarrying, with the Pastors and ministers, and it didn't happen for me that way. But I went over my girlfriend's apartment (now my wife), and I was expressing to her my frustration. She prayed for me and, without effort, I was filled. From that moment, I had help. He helped guide my decisions of what to take and what not to. When I built this relationship with the Holy Spirit, I started to outgrow fear and I had accountability. For one thing, He would educate me in the places that I would go. I'm not saying most musicians aren't saved, but I know most have not been baptized in the Holy Spirit. This is a KEY component to keeping yourself on the road, both in secular and in gospel. 'Cause, contrary to popular belief, I've seen just as much dirt in the gospel industry as I have in the secular. The difference is the Holy Spirit. And also I had friends to help with accountability who were filled as well.

AP: You've worked with some of the most renowned Christian recording artists in the world. Was there ever a moment where you were overwhelmed or surprised by your success?

PB: I'm surprised every day that I get to do this. And even after 16 years in the industry, I'm still shocked when some artists know my name. When I first got a personal call from Israel, I laughed because I couldn't believe he knew who I was. Or when Myron Butler approached me to work with him. I was humbled by the opportunity to work with some of the best.

AP: Do you relate to other musicians working in secular music? What are the differences between working in Christian and secular music arenas?

PB: Yes sir. Coming up in Philly, I've been around the secular scene a lot. Most musicians in the secular arena are church boys/girls. We all have similar roots. I've played secular for years and did a lot of recordings as well before God called me out. But He didn't call me out for a rebuke, but for an assignment. A lot of people misjudge how God will use you and where he'll send you. I understand the guys out there who are working to feed their families, but I also know that road (Christian or secular) is not good for some guys at all.

The differences in the industries is like being amongst family (Christian) and then going out into college or the adult world (secular). There is a safety net in the Christian industry, even though some abuse this privilege. In the secular arena, there is very little to no accountability and there's this NO JUDGEMENT ZONE out there that really says that ANYTHING GOES and YOU CAN'T SAY ANYTHING TO ME! So it can be dangerous. Most guys won't admit it, but I've seen both sides intimately. But the key to both worlds is a healthy relationship with the Holy Spirit and some friends to hold you accountable.

AP: Do you feel you have a platform/influence on other musicians based on your success? If so, how do you use that influence?

PB: Absolutely. Like I said earlier, when I started playing with Tye and GA, my influence jumped immediately just due to the influence Tye had. Of course, over time, I had to develop and become worthy of that influence until I could stand on my own two feet and give back. The way I use the influence is I keep my door open wide enough to let some of my base in. I've always been an advocate of answering emails, commenting on social media, and talking to people at engagements. The person I'm talking to determines who I allow closer access. Like, for instance, you can always read when someone is genuine. Sometimes, I'll see me in somebody and extend a hand further to connect. But ultimately, I love teaching the intangibles and things of the Spirit because that's where my greatest growth has come from. Technical knowledge is much [more] easily attained. And I still do share on that front, but my real value is in the intangibles. I always have a younger guy I'm pouring into in most seasons of my life. But these guys always have a sense of humility and purpose. You can't teach someone who isn't ready to be taught. So being teachable and humble is key in mentorship.

AP: Tell us about your family. What do you do to keep your priorities as a husband and father in perspective?

PB: Earlier, I stated that my wife helped me receive the baptism. So of course, the Holy Spirit led me to her to marry after that. Lol. After God, my wife and children are priority, even over the church. Old school teaching sometimes would have you put family after church. No sir. The church is made up of family. Family first. My wife and I have been married 11 years, and I have two boys, 6 and 4. Once I got into the family season, my focus changed from trying reach success to rewarding success. My family is my success. Everything else is benefits, but the job is the family. So when I take a gig or job, it has to be in context with the assignment of my family. I'm now an example to my boys for how to tread forward, and my wife is my co-laborer, not just romance partner. The quality of my gigs have had to match the quality of my family and that tone set by the Holy Spirit. And believe [me], I'm so far from perfect. Sometimes I want to quit, because, as a musician, I see the gigs that are paying the best and have to say no because it will compromise my marriage and family. I heard a great speaker say once, "Before you start climbing the ladder of success, make sure your ladder is on the right building." It was a statement saying to determine what you value before you start your journey.

AP: As you began to work and minister on major projects, how did it affect your family life?

PB: I finally got to a place [where] I realized that success is not about attaining things or awards, but it's about becoming. So every project and job will challenge the inward things. Like, for instance, I can take a real demanding job, and it can consume my time and take away from me and [my] wife. She'll start complaining about us personally. At that point, my attitude is going to be challenged, and in those moments you are tested to see how you've grown. And if you haven't, your response can be very immature, because you can make the job more important or you can remember the real mission. Be a better example to my children so that they have a fighting chance. I have a saying: "If David's father (Saul [symbolically]) would have fought Goliath, then David wouldn't have had to." Some fights can be won before we enter the ring. And that's my job as a father. So, I set boundaries and talk to my wife prior, so that there's an understanding. But I don't get it right most of the time.

AP: Did you ever experience strain between your career and your relationships at home? If so, how did you deal with them?

PB: Absolutely. Usually, when I've taken on a gig and not been led, then I'll usually catch hell. Lol. And even sometimes when I've been led I've caught hell, because that's part of the challenge. Remember, success is about growing not getting. So sometimes I'll try to move forward in ministry (my own ventures) and hit a bump in the road, because I didn't pour into my wife and kids adequately prior to. So, they'll cry for my attention and compete with my ministry, because they haven't been ministered to yet. With my wife, it can just be me speaking the word to her or a date night, and with my boys, it's about quality time. So, everything is a lesson in becoming. My marriage isn't perfect, but it's growing and that's the key. Not perfection, but growth. Sometimes traveling gets to be too much for the family, so there were times I had to sacrifice money and trust the Holy Spirit to help me come up with ways to provide. A lot of my peers in the game feel like I should be doing more and [taking] the crazy big gigs (Pop / Hip Hop / R&B), because they think just making money will solve my problems. Some of those aren't married today because of wrong values. And it's not a judgment against them, but an observation. I've been in some low places in my career, and God has sustained me because I was willing to grow, and my wife with me.

AP: If there was one piece of advice you could give a young musician starting out, what would it be?

PB: Before you do anything, seek the Holy Spirit. Get filled and build a relationship with him. He will guide you, and sometimes it won't be where you think or even where you want to go. You'll go against the crowd most times, but I promise you there's no safer place to be. This thing is real. All of the other stuff will be added. That comes from my favorite scripture, Matthew 6:33; *But seek first (not only) the kingdom of God and his righteousness and all these things* *shall be added unto you.* You don't have to CHASE what will be added if you seek the Kingdom first.

Chapter Six

Respect the Business

Music is spiritual. The music business is not.

- Van Morrison

A local TV reporter is in your area doing a story on the music scene. She walks up to some people that have worked with you and asks a probing question. "What is like to work with (your name)?" What will they say? Is this an interview that you want to appear on your local news, or do you hope that they cut away to a story on a waterskiing dog or the new vegan diner opening downtown?

If you are worried about what people say about you publicly, you've already got a problem. Even if your name isn't appearing on TV, it is appearing within private conversations among your colleagues, whether you are aware of it or not. They may be describing you with words like talented, gifted, amazing, or expressive. Unfortunately, they could also be using words like chronically late, greedy, unprofessional, and arrogant. Your career will only thrive if the second set of words is inaccurate.

Although many musicians are pleasant and professional, our collective reputation suffers every time a musician demonstrates a lack of integrity. As a result, those performers who are on time, good team players, and doing their best in every working environment have to maintain a high level of consistency to avoid being lumped in with the stereotypical, selfish, and unreliable musician.

The toughest part about being a musician is that much of the job is not about music. Your ability to work with others is just as, if not more, important than your skill. Your success or failure depends on how you handle the business aspects of your career. We'll focus on the professional issues that apply to both religious and popular performances.

THREE ELEMENTS OF PROFESSIONALISM

First we need a working definition of professionalism. Merriam Webster defines 'professionalism', in part, as "Characterized by or conforming to the technical or ethical standards of a profession: exhibiting a courteous, conscientious, and generally businesslike manner in the workplace." No matter what level of skill you possess, you did not acquire it by simply looking at an instrument and willing yourself into playing. At some point, you decided to practice. The same applies to your professional reputation. You cannot simply hope to become a respected musician without practicing ethical behavior and proper etiquette toward your clients, church or colleagues.

Some musicians believe that once you are paid to perform, you become a professional. That may be technically accurate, but it's not the true measure of a professional. If you are not exhibiting the qualities listed above consistently, it doesn't matter how many tours, albums, or stages you have performed on. You are not really a professional until your conduct and performances are consistent in three areas: presentation, preparation, and punctuality.

1. Presentation - This is how you look and how you sound. While many musicians may think only their playing matters, a great performance is negated if it's given in a sloppy or inappropriate package. Every booking should be preceded by a simple question – "What should I wear?" If the event calls for black tie, that is not the time to try out your paisley or plaid ensemble. Your talent will not help you keep a position if you don't look the part. Playing the music with skill and effectiveness must be accompanied by a confident and professional appearance.

2. Preparation – You must learn the material before the gig (not on the way to it), and have the proper equipment at all times. Clearly, there is no excuse for arriving at a gig without having learned the music. In the same way, there is nothing more frustrating to a band or music director than to have to wait for a musician who cannot find a cable, music stand, or other essential equipment. Imagine a doctor without a stethoscope or gloves, or a technician arriving at your house with no tools. You would never hire those individuals again. Don't be the musician who has great knowledge but poor organizational habits.

3. Punctuality - Being on time and punctual is never an option. Timeliness should never be an issue for musicians who have the privilege of performing for a living. So many musicians wish that they had an opportunity to have this blessing. Yet, for many bands and musicians, punctuality, or lack of, is a constant issue. Being late implies that you aren't very serious about keeping your opportunity. Punctual means arriving early enough to set up equipment! The start time for events is NEVER the time that the musician should arrive. If you consistently ignore this responsibility, don't be surprised if your gig opportunities dwindle.

All three of these categories apply to any genre of music, and, if applied consistently, will result in a career that fellow musicians and clients will respect. Gaining respect from others is an indispensable characteristic for any professional.

If you lose it, you will have a hard time surviving in this business.

MIND YOUR BUSINESS: CHURCH AND GIGS

While the ministry of the Church is not a business, the administration of the music ministry is a cauldron of potential business conflicts. Pastors and church leaders often employ musicians to work in their ministries, and that means position requirements, compensation, and other employment issues have to be discussed and agreed to. When the musicians and church leaders are in harmony, it can be a beautiful partnership. When they are not, it can be as painful as a divorce. We have to recognize how fragile this relationship is, and handle it with care, both spiritually and professionally. Every agreement, contract, and guideline between a musician and a church should be in writing, just like it would be in any other workplace. To ignore the need for integrity and transparency in negotiations between musicians and churches is to show a lack of respect for the special place music has in corporate worship and in God's kingdom. Moreover, the absence of a contract invites confusion and chaos, which can wreck the testimony and effectiveness of the church from the top down.

Both musicians and church leaders must be willing to be honorable and fair when resolving contractual and employment issues. If you need help in this area, look for resources on music ministry and church administration. Investing time and energy into the partnership between church and musician can go a long way in avoiding the damage done when pastors and worship musicians can't agree.

HANDLING SCHEDULING CONFLICTS

If you work in a church and do other gigs, it's only a matter of time before you run into schedule conflicts. I'm pretty sure you can guess what the key word is in dealing with these conflicts. That's right. Communication. Insert your 'Captain Obvious' look here.

While it may seem trite and tiresome, it's true. Communicating with everyone in your circle is the key to handling conflicting schedules. I've yet to see a situation end negatively when a musician clearly communicated with all parties involved. By respecting the needs of the church as well as the needs of the industry, we can successfully balance sometimes competing interests. On the other hand, I've seen time and time again where a loss of communication has created a lack of respect and a breakdown in the relationship between a musician, a church, and a band where all parties feel cheated and wronged. It can't be emphasized enough; honesty and timely communication are the ultimate signs of respect.

The question of which event to choose when church and gigs collide can't be answered with one catch-all criteria. It all comes back to priorities. Ministry should always be one of our highest priorities. However, that does not mean that every church event must take priority over a gig. Like all other professions, we have job requirements that sometimes must take precedence over a particular church event. Providing for our families is our first priority, and just as God can bless us for serving God's house, he can also bless us for maintaining our commitment to a work assignment, especially when we've given our word to be there. Scripture tells us to speak the truth to our neighbors (Zechariah 8:16). Don't turn serving God into an excuse for not honoring your word. Be clear and consistent with your commitments. Let people know your needs and schedules as early as possible so that there will be no resentment. Respect the time and resources of those you play with and for.

Advice from the Pros

People don't know that we spend time on the tour bus mapping out six weeks' worth of music [for the church]. I've literally been backstage at an arena while people are sound checking, on the phone, trying to see what's going on in choir rehearsal.

- Dwayne Bennett

Once a written agreement is reached, it is now up to you to protect your reputation and the reputation of all musicians by keeping your part of the agreement. No amount of talent can make up for a lack of integrity. Issues of integrity include punctuality, respect for authority, and attention to detail. Each time a musician doesn't respect the boundaries of an agreement, a fracture appears between the performer and the client. These fractures take a long time to heal, and can cause a permanent limp in your career. I am willing to guess that 90% of all problems between musicians and their clients have nothing to do with music and everything to do with communication and agreements. Respecting the business means always doing everything, if not more, than what is required in the agreement. Learning all the music, keeping equipment ready and prepared, and showing up early is the minimum.

Equally as important as being prepared is having the right mindset when you show up. There are few professions where people depend on each other as much in an ensemble, and one's ability to make a band or event go smoothly is a skill worth its weight in gold. Maintaining a professional and pleasant attitude is the key to enjoying long-term success in this business. People want to work with musicians that make work easy.

KNOWING THE DIFFERENCE BETWEEN PERFORMANCE AND MINISTRY

Although there are similarities between church business and the gig business, there are also very clear differences. Ministries differ in their needs, style of worship, and their production approach, but usually the church musician is not supposed to be the center of attention. On the other hand, there are several popular genres where showmanship is expected on the stage. It is a painfully awkward situation when a church musician draws all the attention to herself behind the pulpit. My advice: don't mix performance with ministry! When a musician brings an entertainment persona onto the ministry platform, it almost always sours the atmosphere and creates a rift that makes congregations and pastors distrust all musicians. When you respect the difference between the two worlds, you are more likely to be treated with respect in both areas.

Think of it this way. If a media team member in a church started running advertisements for their own company on the screens, that person would be removed immediately. A worship musician that plays a gig-style performance is essentially doing the same thing. There is only one entity that should be glorified in a worship service, and that is God himself. Always respect the difference between worship services and your outside performances.

PREPARATION IS NOT OPTIONAL

There is, however, one similarity between gigs and worship music settings. Both require preparation. Far too many times, musicians in the church believe that playing for God means that preparation is optional. Nothing could be further from the truth. Serving God through music requires that we prepare and rehearse our craft in order to give God our best. A cavalier attitude toward preparation doesn't belong in any professional sphere of music, and certainly not in worship. Furthermore, it is embarrassing to other church musicians who have to deal with the stereotype of the person who 'wings it' every Sunday.

As one of my colleagues succinctly stated, "The answer is to learn the music!" It doesn't matter if you have played a certain song a thousand times. Listen and practice it again each time you are scheduled to play it. When an artist or a performer sends a track list, study and rehearse the music so that you can perform it accurately. In 2 Timothy 2:15, Paul commands Timothy, "Be diligent to present yourself approved to God." While Paul was referring to the study of the Word, this principle also applies to musicians. When we prepare properly with the right spirit, God smiles on our performances.

RESPECT THE STYLE

Every style of music has a unique combination of melody, rhythm, and harmony. Great musicians know it's important to recognize and respect the uniqueness of each genre. Avoid thinking that you can mix styles. For example, a rhythm and blues song and a gospel song may have similar chords, but the small differences in style make a big impact. Sometimes, we can put too much of our own preferred style into music that doesn't call for it. Maybe we are accustomed to using church style chord progressions, but when we play a Top 40 gig, those progressions don't fit. Professionals know they have to match the style that is called for in the performance. Be sensitive to the unique aspects of each genre of music you are asked to play, and by all means, listen, listen, listen until you understand what makes that style unique.

DEALING WITH RELATIONSHIPS

As we practice professional behavior in our business practices and performances, we must also handle our relationships professionally. If we have healthy relationships, our music will reflect it. If our relationships are strained, the tension will eventually seep into our sound. Of course, every partnership will have ups and downs. But without good relationship skills, your career will not prosper the way it should. You can try to maintain a career on talent alone, but it will likely be accompanied by relational brokenness and unnecessary personal turmoil.

"People don't care how much you know, until they know how much you care" is just as true in the music industry as anywhere else. There is no substitute for genuine care and respect for people, whether they can do something for you professionally or not. When artists share a common goal, it can lead to great achievements. Just look at the some of the successful partnerships in music history: Rodgers and Hammerstein, Ellington and Strayhorn, Gamble and Huff, Quincy Jones and Michael Jackson, and so on. There is nothing more powerful in music than a group of talented people uniting to create something special.

A relationship is always built on two things: mutual respect and trust. Trust is equally as important as respect in every musician's lifestyle. In fact, one might say the currency of relationship is trust. If you have a lot of it, your relationship is rich. If there is no trust, the relationship is poor and probably in danger of collapsing. You have to know how and why to build up this account of trust. Don't be the musician who tries to make a withdrawal from a relationship account that has been in the red for years due to negligence. You need to be intentional about building trust.

TWO KINDS OF TRUST

Whether on the stage or behind the pulpit, musical trust is the glue that holds a performance together. It means everyone is playing with the intent to make the group sound better. When musicians play with a selfish attitude and ignore the overall purpose of the ensemble, trust is broken. Trusting each other during a performance means:

- Listening to each other.
- Knowing the music well.
- Not playing over each other.
- Blending as an ensemble.

- Watching for cues and being aware of changes.
- Playing the part as written and rehearsed.

A musician can strengthen relationships by employing these skills consistently at every rehearsal and performance. When your bandmates see and sense these skills from you, it develops a sense of trust, and leads not only to better music performances, but better relationships off the stage. Without these skills, you'll find your fellow musicians are less willing to work with you. On the other hand, by playing your part skillfully and making the ensemble sound better, you can quickly establish a solid working relationship with other musicians.

While trust on stage requires musical intelligence, trust off the stage requires emotional intelligence. Treating your colleagues with respect shows that you can be trusted to be a musician of integrity. These relationship skills include:

- Punctuality to all events and rehearsals.
- Respecting the bandleader's authority.
- Always responding promptly to communication.
- Handling financial issues professionally.
- Respecting other's work by not stealing gigs or opportunities from other musicians.

○ Refusing to gossip about other musicians.

No matter how respectful you try to be, however, relationship conflicts will sometimes occur, whether they are artistic arguments, personality problems between musicians, or business-related disagreements. In any of these cases, you can be firm and professional in your interactions without being harsh or unlikable. "Letting your no mean no, and your yes mean yes," (Matt. 5:37) will build respect and trust among your colleagues, especially since integrity and consistency are rare in entertainment circles.

As a Christian, you have an even higher standard than your peers in your treatment of others. In Romans 12:18, the apostle Paul tells us, "If it is possible, as much as depends on you, live peaceably with all men." If anyone ever had a legitimate reason to fight back, it was Paul. He was abused and mistreated continuously, but he valued his Christian witness more than his pride. Sometimes, you will have to be a peacemaker, even while you deal with tough issues and difficult people. Do your best to help settle conflicts rather than ignite them.

Allen C. Paul

DIFFERENCE BETWEEN 'CLIQUES' AND 'CIRCLES'

Every musician needs a team of supporters. Usually, a few close friends become the partners you depend on. We could call this group your inner circle. They may be the band members, producers, or friends that you call first for help and advice. You probably also prefer to work with them when you are given a choice. It's natural to be loyal to those who assist you professionally and personally. However, if your circle begins to exhibit an attitude of superiority over those outside the circle, you may be creating a clique. Rather than helping your career, cliques make relationship building more difficult.

Jesus demonstrated how a healthy inner circle functions with his three closest disciples, Peter, James, and John. Jesus spent much more time and shared more information with them, knowing they would one day be leaders of the early church. In the same way, your inner circle should consist of people who share your vision and your desire to succeed. However, the Pharisees and Sadducees saw themselves as greater than everyone else. Their primary goal was not to promote care and concern for each other, but to *demote and belittle* anyone not sharing their views.

Your circle should be a source of professional support. It should not be a wall between you and your fellow musicians. It's okay to have a close-knit circle of friends. Just remember to keep an open door policy for those who are genuinely willing to support you, and you will avoid the pitfalls of cliquish behavior.

> ### Advice from the Pros

In most churches, we believe the highest pinnacle of skill is playing in the church, but there are higher degrees of faithfulness. It's God that raises one up and puts down another. If God increases you to another level, [you] have to learn to release [your previous assignment]. When we release that, we allow the next faithful person to come up through the ranks.

- Khristian Dentley

MAINTAIN PROFESSIONAL BOUNDARIES

While it's a blessing to work with partners we know and trust, it's important to maintain professional boundaries, even when working within your circle. When we don't clarify expectations and agreements, close relationships can be damaged and feelings hurt. Any time money, time, or services are exchanged, there should be a written agreement between the parties involved. Even if your church, band, or partners have worked together for years, respect every agreement as if you were strictly business associates. Otherwise, there is the possibility of losing both a business connection and a personal friend over things that really don't matter in the long run.

WHEN RELATIONSHIPS GO BAD

Not every relationship is designed to last forever. Some partnerships end when both parties realize that they have new ideas and visions that cannot be maintained simultaneously. Hopefully the individuals can go their separate ways on good terms. However, sometimes this isn't the case, and a messy break-up can ensue. It's very important to recognize the signs of an eroding partnership and make every effort to avoid unnecessary conflicts and personal attacks. When you find yourself in an adversarial position, remember that being righteous may be more important than being right. Being righteous requires humility and patience, even when you are being treated unfairly. If you are able to maintain your professional reputation and integrity in a matter where a band or partnership has to end, you can walk away without regret, even when the other party may not share the same feelings.

While it's easy to blame others when conflicts arise, be willing to acknowledge that you may be part of the problem. As artists, we can sometimes become selfish in our pursuit of success. Consider how the book of James diagnoses the cause of relational conflicts; *What causes fights and quarrels among you? Don't they come from your desires that battle within you?* (James 4:1).

The Bible points out that it is our desire to get our way that prevents us from seeking peace and reconciliation. Any time we are more focused on how we can win a relational conflict, rather than finding the best solution, we're part of the problem. The correct response to broken relationships is always to communicate more, pray more, and actively seek solutions that will glorify God and respect others. For more information on handling conflict, I recommend Ken Sande's book, "The Peacemaker".

DEALING WITH NEGATIVE RELATIONSHIPS

Sometimes relationships in music are adversarial from the start. I wish all musicians were helpful and kind, but that's not reality. Some musicians are overly competitive, territorial, mistrusting, and sometimes downright mean. Those who don't aspire to the same ethics as you may try to undermine your reputation and make your career more difficult. What should be your response when you face opposition from your peers?

You must keep the same attitude that Job had when he faced accusers; he maintained his integrity. Don't resort to pettiness and drama when you could be focused on improving yourself and creating new music. Remaining true to your art and your ethics is the only way to respond. Your actions speak louder than your words. Instead of striking back at your enemies, respond like David did when he saw the unrighteous prospering. *When I pondered to understand this, it was troublesome in my sight; until I came into the sanctuary of God; then I perceived their end* (Psalms 73:16-17 NASB).

When David was tempted to focus on how his enemies seemed to be getting away with evil, he went back to what he knew best. He focused on worship. That is when he remembered that those who dishonor God by ignoring his principles are sure to fail. Material success does not equal eternal reward. Do your best to refrain from engaging in complaining about others that don't play fair. Be honest if you have to discuss a negative event during a gig or performance, but don't take the opportunity to bash a fellow musician. Let God fight that battle as you stand firm in your faith and your calling.

ACCEPT THE CHALLENGE

Dealing with the music business can be a struggle, but it's also an opportunity to let God's light shine in an industry that desperately needs more truth, love, and honesty. Each challenge you face is another chance to demonstrate how God blesses those who honor his principles. Don't run from the challenge. Embrace an attitude of excellence, so you can enjoy the resulting blessings in your daily work.

CHAPTER SEVEN

Visualize your Goals

It is not a lack of spiritual experience that leads to failure, but a lack of working to keep our eyes focused and on the right goal... like a musician who gives no thought to audience approval, if he can only catch a look of approval from his Conductor.

- Oswald Chambers

You've gone from dreaming about a music career to actually pursuing one. You've felt the urge to step out and make a mark in the local scene or perform extensively with other bands for the first time. Maybe you've decided to step forward and join the praise and worship team at your church. Perhaps you want to record your first album or enter your first songwriting competition. You've decided to take a leap of faith. That big first step may be the hardest one to make, but it must be followed by a lot of little steps. Where do you begin?

A working musician has to have a plan. Plenty of people dream of success, but few develop a strategy to reach their goals. No one becomes a star by sitting around and waiting for a lucky break. Even prayer and positive confessions aren't effective if they are not accompanied by preparation. The Word tells us that faith without works is dead (James 2:26). In regards to reaching your goals, you could paraphrase that verse like this: Dreaming of success without taking action is pointless.

This quote, attributed to speaker Greg Reid, sums up the process of moving from the dream stage into real action. *"A dream written down with a date becomes a goal. A goal broken down into steps becomes a plan. A plan backed by action makes your dreams come true."* This process of turning your dreams into a plan is what we call visualizing your goals.

The visualization process has two parts, creating and refining the vision for your career and presenting your vision to others.

SEE THE VISION

When you became a musician, your goal was probably simple; to play your instrument anywhere and everywhere there was an opportunity. Thankfully, though we live in a time where technology often replaces live talent, there are still many opportunities available for the performing musician. Restaurants and clubs still seek out live music acts to improve the atmosphere of their establishments. Live music concerts continue to be popular, and thousands of music fans attend festivals all over the country. Artists everywhere are seeking out fresh sounds and top-notch musicians to help create the next big hit. There are opportunities for musicians in studios that produce films, television shows, video games, commercials, and web-based entertainment.

As for churches, many ministries still struggle to find qualified musicians. This need will continue to grow as more and more congregations incorporate contemporary worship services that require trained and prepared musicians. However, a musician can't simply plan to land the perfect gig or the perfect church assignment. Your dream of making music will not occur by accident. You must design a plan to reach it.

WRITE IT DOWN

In the chase for gigs, it's easy to focus on the next paycheck, the next opportunity, or the next performance. That type of focus can be helpful for short-term goals, but it's not good when you consider your long-term vision. That great opportunity you come across, if not compatible with the vision for your career, can eventually become a burden rather than a blessing. As Aaron Lindsey remarked, "The place you romanticize may become the place of responsibility."[3] Perhaps you have promised yourself that songwriting will be your focus, and yet you spend hours doing other artists' music and neglecting your own creative gift. How can you keep the hustle of musician life from overwhelming your long-term goals?

The answer is to visualize what you want your career to look like and write it down. This is commonly known as a vision statement. You've probably seen one in your workplace, church, or any other organization that has a specific mission or focus. The vision statement sets the parameters and priorities that will guide the decisions of an individual or an organization. There are myriad examples of vision statements in self-help and career books if you need a template. I have included my current vision statement below. It has been revised several times over the years, and I will continue to revise it throughout my career.

I am a follower of Christ, a man of principle who maintains his physical health, a husband who loves his wife, a

---

[3] November 11th, 2014 "414 Ministries" Prayer Conference Call

dad who cherishes his kids, and a giver who chooses wealth over debt.

Through innovative teaching methods, personal coaching, and writing, I lead and teach 400 people every year to have more confidence in their God-given artistic ability. I express the excellence of God's creativity through my musical performances, and I create new ideas and music frequently by connecting with highly motivated and talented artists.

To determine your vision, first return to the second step in our S.E.R.V.I.C.E. model and write down what your priorities are. If God has called you to a career in music, you then have to write down exactly what that means in practical terms.

ANSWER THESE QUESTIONS IN YOUR VISION STATEMENT:

- What is the focus of my career?
- What will I create?
- Where will I perform, teach, mentor, compose?
- Who is my target audience?
- How many projects/performances do I want to participate in?

After you answer the questions above in your vision statement, you then have to plan the steps to reach each goal you have set. This may be done in a business plan format, by writing deadlines on a calendar, or even an informal checklist. The key is to get your thoughts on paper, where they can be evaluated, re-evaluated, and put into action.

When a business wants to know what they have available to sell, they take inventory of their current products. In the same way, when you want to know how you can reach your musical and personal goals, you must take personal inventory of your gifts and talents, your resources, and your connections.

CONSIDER MAKING A LIST OF:

- Equipment/Instruments you already have.
- Your skills/abilities/strengths.
- Your financial resources.
- People/Professional networking relationships you can tap into.
- Venues/Churches you have worked with.
- Supporters/Fans/Family that will help you.

Taking inventory of what you already have can be an eye-opening exercise. Many musicians assume that the resources they need are far beyond their reach, when there may actually be opportunities and resources that are easily accessible.

Taking inventory is an important part of mapping out a successful strategy.

One strategy is to start your project planning from the end, and work your way backwards. If your goal is to produce an album, then start from the album's release date and think of what you need to do one week before, two weeks before, a month before, etc., until you reach your current point. That will show you the timetable you have to stick to in order to reach your goal.

CHARTING YOUR COURSE

I also suggest that every working musician create a priorities chart – one that states your career goals and your priorities in visual form. Write down what's important to you; your family, your church, and your career. Then write down how you will prioritize the choices that involve each area of your life. Visualize what you would do if faced with a choice between two good options, so that when that moment comes, you already know where your priorities lie.

Creating this chart can help you turn dream scenarios into a practical strategy. For example, what would you do if you got a call from a big-time artist that wants you to tour? How would you handle it? What steps would you have to take? How would your priorities of church or family be affected? Consider and then write down the path you would take in this situation. Of course, you can't see the future, but this is both an exercise in faith and a practical way of planning your career. By visualizing your choices before they are presented to you, a foundation that will help you achieve your ultimate goals is set.

FROM VISION TO PROMOTION

Once you have completed a vision statement and a set of goals, you then have to make those goals public. No one can follow a vision that they are unaware of. This is the art of promotion, bringing others into your vision and making them a part of it. The businesses we now know as iconic brands started as a vision; Steve Jobs and Apple, Ray Kroc and McDonalds, Mark Zuckerberg and Facebook. Each of these visionaries had to make their vision attractive to those who would help to make it a reality. Even Jesus had to step out of the anonymity of Nazareth to proclaim the gospel. As he began his ministry, he chose twelve common men to help him spread his message. He was God's Son, yet he couldn't carry the vision of the Kingdom by himself. In the same way, every musician, even those who perform behind the scenes, must utilize the power of promotion.

Allen C. Paul

PROMOTION VERSUS PRIDE

The art of promotion is very familiar to those in advertising and the corporate world, but those of us in religious circles are sometimes told that promoting ourselves is selfish. You may feel that promoting your dreams publicly brings glory to you instead of God. While it is true that some musicians and artists become obsessed with their brand, this doesn't mean promotion is a bad thing. It means that promotion must be paired with humility. Humility means thinking no more or less of yourself than what God thinks of you. If you are wary of pride overtaking you, that is good news. Pride is a silent killer. Often, prideful people are deaf to the warning signs. By maintaining a consistent prayer life and an awareness of the danger of pride, you will be less likely to give in to a selfish attitude. You can then sincerely promote your vision without solely seeking the approval of others.

Wait, you ask, doesn't promotion require you to look for approval and support from others? Yes, that is part of promotion. However, you should never depend on outside approval in order to validate your vision. If you are only motivated by the approval of others, your audience becomes your master, rather than the Spirit of God. Always remember that your ultimate purpose is to fulfill God's vision for your life, not your own. Without that understanding, the desire for approval might become the fuel that feeds a 'me-first' mentality.

BE CONFIDENT IN YOUR VISION

There will only be one you in all of human history, and your unique ability can never be duplicated. Your story and your creative spirit are valuable assets. They are God's gift to you, so don't be ashamed when you share your vision with others. Don't use phrases such as "it's just a little thing", "it's a hobby", "maybe it will work", etc. Speak with a confident attitude when it comes to your career and your abilities. People can read your body language and expression even more clearly than they can hear your words. If you are shy, reluctant, or dismissive about your own vision, there's little chance your potential supporters will see hope for success. Whether it is an interview, rehearsal, performance, or just meeting new people, always remember to share your vision with passion and confidence. You never know who might support your goals and make your success their top priority.

DON'T BE SCARED TO SHARE

Sharing your story can be scary, especially when other musicians are in direct competition with you. You also may feel that promoting yourself invites criticism from others. It's true; dealing with negativity is a part of the business you will have to accept. Remember Joseph's story from the Bible. His problems began when he shared his dreams with his brothers, but he continued to believe in the vision God had for his life. If your gift or talent is leading you toward bigger things, you have to have a prayerful but confident attitude that you are on the right path. If you are worried about other people stealing your ideas, you're probably in the wrong business. The music business is a copy-cat industry. If you are successful, you will likely be imitated! In fact, sharing your dreams might inspire others to reach for their goals.

The Bible clearly states in Proverbs 29:15 that the "fear of man" is a trap that keeps us from seeing everything that God has for us. If your success is a God-given goal, then trust God to bring it to pass, and don't be overcome with worry or anxiousness about how people will respond to you.

FULL-TIME PROMOTER, PART-TIME MUSICIAN

I've joked with many of my musician friends that once I finished school, I stopped being a musician and became a full-time promoter of my music. The challenge of promoting yourself means dealing with the crowd of artists doing the same thing. It seems that everyone has a website, a YouTube video, and a new single on Soundcloud or Spotify. How can you stand out?

To do this, you must establish your brand. . A musical brand is the foundation from which your creative decisions arise. This doesn't mean you shouldn't be able to re-invent yourself and perform in several different styles. It's how you approach each piece and each performance. It's what makes you sound different from other musicians who play the same instrument. Without a brand, you're a carbon copy of someone else's creativity.

Forming a brand takes time. Miles Davis said, "It took a long time to sound like myself." Every musician begins their studies by learning from the masters, but when the skills and sounds you learn from others are woven into your own life experience, you begin to form your own sound. That identity is the unique trait that artists, producers, bands and churches look for when they hire musicians. They don't just look for talent. They also look for musicians who fit their identity. If you are unsure of your own identity, you can't connect it with others.

Once you have developed your brand, be consistent. Whether you promote yourself through the web, print media, resumes, or other means, make the message of your music easy to grasp for everyone that you connect with professionally.

One method of quickly sharing your brand and your vision is the twenty second commercial, or elevator pitch. Can you share what you do and what you are trying to achieve in twenty seconds or less? If not, you haven't effectively broken down your vision so that someone unfamiliar with your work can understand and support you.

NETWORKING WITH THOSE THAT HAVE BEEN THERE

The Bible says, "there is safety in having many advisers." (Proverbs 11:14 NLT). In practical terms, to see whether your vision is achievable, share it with other musicians who have gone where you want to go. While the music business has changed drastically over the last few decades, the steps to becoming a competent musician have not. One of the best resources you can have is a relationship with an experienced and successful colleague. There's no need to struggle on your own if other people can help you avoid the pitfalls that they endured.

To do this, be willing to humble yourself, ask questions, and sometimes accept rejection. Not every experienced artist has a mentoring mindset. In my experience, however, successful musicians are glad to share their story. They likely learned from someone in their season of growth, and they appreciate the honor and responsibility of helping other upcoming musicians.

As you search for connections and mentoring relationships, be careful not to rely on name-dropping or relationships that are developed with ulterior motives. There is nothing wrong with making connections with successful people. The problem arises when you try to base your success on those connections *alone.* No one is impressed when you simply list a bunch of famous names. People will hire you based on your attitude and your ability, not your contact list. Just knowing the right people is not enough. You also have to be the *right kind of person* yourself. Be a person that demonstrates humility and integrity, and you'll attract the opportunities you desire.

ALWAYS REMEMBER TO SUPPORT YOUR FELLOW ARTISTS

Philippians 2:3 - 4 states, "Do nothing out of selfish ambition or vain conceit. Rather, in humility value others above yourselves, not looking to your own interests but each of you to the interests of the others." This verse highlights our duty to put others' needs above our own. Unfortunately, some of us do not follow this principle. Instead, we see the music world as a pie and compete to take the biggest slice, even if it means cutting others out. This is the wrong way to build relationships. The best way to improve your professional opportunities is to promote and support others in your field; a rising tide lifts all. When musicians are able to support and encourage excellence in each other, we increase our influence in the culture and improve our reputation in the industry. There will always be competition for the eyes and ears of the public, but that competition does not have to foster resentment between the artists in the local scene themselves. Big record companies and other national entities have to fight for market share and radio time. Local musicians and worship leaders must realize that promoting each other actually helps them individually.

I encourage you to attend and support the performances of your fellow local musicians. Go to their concerts and promote events in your area whenever you can. Promote your colleagues' releases and products. As you build goodwill with your fellow musicians, you are building a framework for your own success.

START THE JOURNEY

And then GOD answered, "Write this. Write what you see. Write it out in big block letters so that it can be read on the run

-Habakkuk 2:2, The Message

You've dreamed of taking your music to new heights, but if you have not written your vision down, it's easy to get lost on the way to your goal. The life of a musician isn't a sprint; it is a cross country race full of turns, hills, and bumps that can cause you to trip and fall. By creating and fine tuning your vision, you continue moving in the direction that God has ordained for your career. Your goals may change over time, but discipline and foresight will help you make adjustments and stay on course.

Tell the friends in your circle to hold you accountable to your deadlines and stated intentions. Make sure your family knows where you are headed and always keep them informed of what steps lie ahead. Above all, talk to God about your plans and speak words of success from the scriptures over yourself. As Ephesians 3:22 tells us, God's plans for us are immeasurably higher than anything we can ask or think. My personal interpretation of this verse is that when we dare to dream big, God is ready and willing to exceed our expectations. But when we refuse to think or ask for great things, God isn't impressed. He's not into low expectations. Godly success comes when you embrace all the possibilities that God has for you to experience.

> ## Conversations With The Pros: James Dawkins

James Dawkins (www.mrjamesdawkins.com) and I have a long history. I first met him while interning as a music education student in his high school band. Later, we served as ministers of music in sister churches, and we have both branched out into full-time music careers. He's worked with local and international artists in both gospel and popular music. I spoke with him about the transition and how he handles the responsibilities of his music career and his ministry.

Allen Paul: How do you decide who will be on your musical team?

James Dawkins: Character is very important. I've recommended guys that made me look bad, and I'll never recommend them again. It's not 100% about skill. I know guys that can (only) play on an entry level, but I put them on my team.

AP: Why do you aspire to be more than an "every Sunday" musician?

JD: My gift was bigger than the four walls of the church. If you do popular music, you get everybody. I wanted to broaden my horizons. We can't be boxed in. Our music has to reach everybody, regardless of religion, race, or ethnicity.

AP: What issues arise with churches work with touring musicians?

JD: Most of the time, when churches hire a good quality musician that's ministry minded, it never occurs to them that they might leave. That's part of the problem of when musicians leave; they [churches] never plan for your departure. Communication between church and musician has to start from the beginning. People reject what they don't understand. My commitment to the church is to find a suitable replacement while I'm gone. I handle the business of paying my replacement so they don't have to worry about that.

AP: How do you prioritize your time to create?

JD: When I think about time, the time that we don't get back...we have to get on the ball, and make a difference. Sometimes, we can get caught up in other things. I want to treat this music thing like my life depends on it. I'm making that vow to myself. The clock is ticking.

AP: How important is your faith while on tour?

JD: I believe that if you have a solid foundation before you get caught up in touring and traveling, then you have a basis to stand on. But if your faith is shaken, you can get lost in the shuffle. I've traveled with guys who do not have the same faith. You have to be rooted and grounded before you ever branch out [to tour]. Our lifestyle is the example.

AP: How do you deal with the competitive mentality between musicians?

JD: I was always confident in my ability to do what I can do. I can only be me; I can't be anybody else. If we took that mindset, everyone would end up better. But if I have a mind to compete with you…that's not a winner's mentality. My strong point may not be yours, and your strong point may not be mine. We all have something to bring to the table. We still share common ground because we're professional musicians.

AP: What would you tell young musicians to change the competitive mentality?

JD: Mostly the younger guys feel like they have a point to prove. You have to prove to them that you have respect from the people that they respect. Most young musicians want to be like people who are on the scene. They tend to respect those people a little bit more. Maturity allows us to keep things in perspective. It's not all about chops. You're an accompanist.

Chapter Eight

Invest in Your Skill

The most important investment you can make is in yourself.

- Warren Buffett

Every farmer knows the importance of planting. It is not enough to have the best soil, great weather, and a multitude of seeds. No successful farmers stare at the field and wait for the crops to spring up. They roll up their sleeves and do the hard work of preparing the ground for a good harvest. No one notices the hard work, but they do notice when the seeds germinate and the fields are full of produce. In the same way, a musician can't expect to be successful by waiting for his or her big break. There must be some work involved, and much of that work will be done in secret. What we might view as an overnight success is usually the result of years of work in the background.

Sometimes, we artists complain that those who have become successful had more help. It's true; some musicians do get a boost from outside sources. But that's not the norm. No one should be more invested in your career than you are. Your ability to thrive as a Christian musician will depend on how deeply you invest in yourself.

While investing time and energy into your career is important, the most pressing issue for many musicians is their financial commitment.

INVESTING IN YOUR TOOLS

Let's admit it; we all love new gear. Having the newest instruments, sounds, software, and gadgets can make any musician as excited as a child on Christmas Day. However, investing in your skill does not mean breaking the bank at Sam Ash or Guitar Center. It means regularly investing the funds you earn back into your career, creating new opportunities from those investments, and repeating the process. If you want your career to grow, you must feed and nurture it with wise buying decisions. It's not what you buy; it's how you use the purchase.

I learned this concept when I got my first keyboard. While keyboards made by Roland and Korg were all the rage in the 90's, my father bought a lesser known model for me. At first, I felt like I would be less respected among my peers, but soon they began asking where I got my unique sounds. It turned out, having a keyboard that few musicians knew about made my performances more recognizable. A key factor in choosing what gear to purchase is not the cost, but rather how much it helps you improve as a performer and artist. You may not need every new shiny gadget that the music superstore is offering you.

However, you should remain familiar with companies, artists, and musicians on the cutting edge of music creation. When the time arrives to buy the new guitar, keyboard, bass, or drum set, you'll want to be ready to put all the advancements to good use in actual performances. A musician's sound is their unique advertisement. If your sound is not up-to-date, it can have a negative impact on your opportunities. Be thoughtful and professional about your equipment choices and you'll see an immediate payoff from your investments.

THE VALUE OF SOUND FINANCIAL ADVICE

If you listen to commercial radio, you've probably noticed certain questionable words have become more accepted on the airwaves over the years. But for many musicians, the most problematic word isn't a curse word. It's the B-word, "Budget". Being financially responsible seems to be a rare quality in musicians and singers. The industry is full of high-profile artists who have gone bankrupt or to prison due to unpaid taxes and financial mismanagement.

At the local level, many musicians manage their income from gig to gig and paycheck to paycheck. While this is a common method for managing personal finances, it's not the best way to run a business. Without careful planning and saving, you'll find it hard to re-invest in your own career. When it comes to budgeting, taxes, and other financial matters, seek advice from trusted sources, such as certified public accountants or licensed financial advisors. Consider purchasing tax preparation software to help calculate your end of year expenses and to avoid getting in trouble with the IRS. Groups like ASCAP, BMI, and Grammy Pro offer financial workshops for musicians and songwriters. To summarize, treat your music business as just that, a business. Set aside some of your gig income for re-investment into your career, so that it becomes self-sustaining over time.

While we're discussing budgets, we have to discuss the issue of debt. While society pushes credit cards as a necessity, Christians have been warned in the Word to watch out for the traps that excessive debt can create. Proverbs tells us that the borrower is a slave to the lender. That means, when you put your name on a credit card or loan application, you're giving away part of your financial freedom as a person and artist. Be very careful not to burden yourself with debts and credit payments in the hope of advancing your career. Excessive debt can hamper your professional progress as well as your financial future.

INVESTING IN YOUR BRAND

A few years ago, a popular soft drink ran a series of ads with the byline 'Image is nothing'. That's not the case in the music industry. Your image is part of your presentation, and as we discussed in Chapter 6, dressing appropriately is part of every musician's job description. Whether you are performing in a large cathedral, a small coffeehouse, or a major concert hall, proper attire is part of your responsibility, and therefore deserves a place in your budget. Purchase clothing that is in style and reflects your professionalism. Never be the exception to the image when appearing on stage. Investing in your look can be the difference in getting a call back and getting passed over.

Not only should your attire stand out, so should your marketing materials. This means you must set aside resources to promote your brand. Business cards, websites, and other promotional materials should make up a portion of your music budget. Recording artists may need a bigger advertising investment in order to promote themselves, including press kits, professional photography, and press releases. Other musicians may only need a website and business cards. Regardless of what type of audience you are trying to reach, you will not do so effectively without investing in your promotional and professional identity. For more ideas on promotion and budgeting for musicians, I recommend "The Savvy Musician" by David Cutler.

INVESTING IN YOUR LEARNING

Investing into continuing your development is equally as important as investing into your equipment. You might prefer to study new material on your own, but I would strongly recommend seeking out a mentor or teacher who is an expert in your field. Every successful artist knows they need people who can take their career to the next level. The benefits you'll experience from these relationships are worth the investment of your time and resources.

Not only should you continue learning from others, but you must also continually improve yourself. One obvious way to continue improving is to constantly expose yourself to new music. I constantly listen to new styles and artists to help boost my creativity. Buying new music keeps me in tune with the ever-changing tides of the cultural landscape. I never want to become so comfortable with my own style that I stop learning and growing. If I stop learning and expanding my worldview, I cease to be a true artist.

ACTION STEPS:

Consider these methods as you continue your musical development:

Earn a post-graduate degree – This option is beneficial for many musicians, especially for those who want to achieve greater influence and respect in the academic world. Completing a master's or doctoral program can propel you into collegiate teaching positions and greater networking opportunities among those that seek musicians with advanced degrees.

Take lessons from another musician – As we discussed earlier, we can all learn something new from another artist, especially one in a field or genre with which you are unfamiliar. Seeking out assistance from other masters in a certain technique or style can make you a much stronger musician overall. For example, I owe my ability to play the Hammond organ to a musician who took the time to explain the instrument to me step by step. It was an invaluable investment of time that paid back dividends in my career as a full-time worship staff musician.

Attend a national conference or workshop – These gatherings of music professionals and artists are high-impact events that provide networking and learning opportunities. Many popular music and worship music conferences offer classes and panels with top artists. Those in music ministry can find resources at conferences like the National Worship Leadership Conference and the Gospel Music Workshop of America. There are also several popular music conferences, like the National Association of Music Merchants annual convention (NAMM), where vendors display the latest in technology, and South by Southwest (SXSW), which showcases upcoming bands and artists. Events like this can provide valuable understanding into current trends. Attending these conferences can benefit you tremendously in the form of networking, knowledge, and insight not available in your local area.

Study online – In the past decade, the amount of tutorial resources online has increased exponentially. Investigate these options carefully. There is a difference between imitating someone on a video and learning how to do what the teacher is demonstrating. Try to find tutorials and learning materials that teach foundational concepts before asking yourself to master advanced or cool techniques. In both church and popular styles, there is a tendency to look for the newest fad or harmonic twist instead of essential and fundamental music theory. Focus on materials that improve your overall understanding of your chosen instrument.

PRACTICE IS STILL A PRIORITY

As for time on the instrument, there is only one substitute for practice, more practice. No amount of instruction, gigging, or listening can replace what many musicians refer to as "shedding". Applying and reviewing the skills of performance must be a part of a musician's everyday life if he or she wishes to reach full potential.

The dirty little secret among professional musicians is that as you get busier, a steady practice routine becomes harder and harder to maintain. The grind of weekly performances and the familiarity of repertoire done over and over can erode any musician's discipline. Personally, I find myself wishing for the days where I was in college, practicing scales on an upright piano in a dark practice room for hours on end. I was more willing to sacrifice time for practice before I had to prepare for weekly performances. Now that I have been gigging for years, I realize the only way to improve my skills is to practice at the same intensity as I did when I was younger. I have limited time to practice, so I have to make that practice time consistent and effective.

Allen C. Paul

My practice strategy consists of three simple parts: warm-up, technique, and repertoire. Warm-up includes basic scales, finger stretches, and other technical exercises that promote physical soundness in my playing. Technique usually involves finding a position, run, or technique that I'm struggling with and repeating it until it is no longer a struggle. Then I work on the upcoming music for my services and performances. Every musician in every genre should have a strategy and purpose behind their practice sessions.

In the midst of a busy working schedule, it is sometimes impossible to find uninterrupted time to practice. When physical practice isn't feasible, mental practice and rehearsal is an appropriate substitute. This doesn't mean just going over the song in your head. Mental practice involves concentrated focus on specific techniques, melodies, and harmonies so that the mind is just as attuned to a perfect performance as your hands, feet, or voice. Working musicians know how valuable this kind of focused mental rehearsal can be. Whether on the road, backstage, or waiting in an airport, successful musicians find ways to mentally sharpen their skills and prepare for the next performance.

STAY ORGANIZED IN REHEARSAL

If you are a freelance musician, you likely perform for several bands, choirs, ensembles, etc., each with different repertoire and song lists. Keeping all those songs and arrangements in memory can prove difficult (especially since many ensembles don't use printed music onstage). A consistent routine is needed to remain organized and prepared for your different gigs and set-lists. Writing down keys, charts, and arrangements is standard practice for music professionals. It's impossible to remember everything in every rehearsal, so keep notes, make recordings, and mark specific details that you can review in your private practice time. Once you begin reviewing your material, always refer to your notes so you do not mistake one ensemble's arrangement for another's.

As a working musician, the temptation is always there to spend less time on familiar material. But taking songs for granted, even if they are repeatedly performed in your church, band, or show, is a dangerous practice. Over time, small mistakes and missed notes become habit, and eventually you find that your performances of that material are not what they are supposed to be. Take the time to review all the material for each service or performance, regardless of how many weeks or months it has been performed. The seeds of disciplined and productive effort produce a harvest of opportunity and success.

INVESTING ALWAYS BRINGS A RETURN

Sowing seeds into your career is an exercise in faith, but it is an exercise every Christian musician must undertake. You have a unique gift as a working musician, and the talents that you have deserve to be nurtured and developed. In the parable of the talents, Jesus disapproves of the servant that sits on his gift and refuses to increase the Master's investment (Matt 25:14-29). If you are blessed to perform, minister, or entertain as a profession, you are expected to make sacrifices and take risks in order to increase the return on the investment of talent that God gave you. When you do so, you will find that the benefits are long-lasting and fulfilling.

Part III:
Your Calling

Chapter Nine

Challenge Yourself to Grow

The most fatal illusion is the settled point of view. Since life is growth and motion, a fixed point of view kills anybody who has one.

- Brooks Atkinson

It may seem that once you've adopted the first 5 steps of the S.E.R.V.I.C.E. model, you should have achieved a measure of professional stability. By staying connected to God and family, establishing priorities, respecting the business, visualizing goals, and investing in your skills, you may feel that all the criteria for being a successful church and gigging musician have been met. Unfortunately, you would be incorrect.

I can't tell you how many times I've heard musicians within and outside the church complain about feeling stuck.

These usually aren't lazy musicians. In fact, usually they are highly skilled, faithful, and dedicated. Yet, despite their attempts to follow all the right steps in their careers, at some point they feel unfulfilled. Perhaps years of dealing with crooked clergy and crotchety choir members makes them question their calling. Maybe the grind of working the same set of local gigs gets discouraging. In each case, talented and blessed musicians feel burned out and want to give up.

So what should these musicians do? Work harder? Pray more? Make more calls? If they have already done all those things, then what? How far should you go in order to fulfill your dreams?

Here is the most controversial part, perhaps, of this model. I believe that if you want to be spiritually and professionally whole, you must first be willing to give up your musical identity. You must challenge yourself to grow beyond being just a musician.

TWO ROLES, ONE SELF

In "Establishing Priorities", we discussed the importance of authenticity. Knowing who you are is a major factor in avoiding burnout in both music ministry and the music industry. Those of us who work in the ministry are asked to fulfill two very different roles. On one hand, you may be a praise leader, minister, or teacher that is focused on your service to God. On the other, you are an artist, entertainer or musician that devotes at least some of that attention to your audience, band, or event. While we've established that these roles don't conflict each other, they do require different mindsets. If you form your identity around your role rather than on your relationship with God, you may find yourself confused about who you really are.

Maybe you've heard of a gospel song sung by the late Daryl Coley, called "When the Music Stops". In it, Coley sings about how he has to live the same life that he sings about on stage, even if he faces despair or doubt. It's a song about authenticity. A lack of personal authenticity is dangerous to your spiritual health. Whether in front of a church or in front of a stage of screaming fans, the musician that wraps her identity around music alone is a target for depression, unhappiness, and emotional turmoil when she separated from that crutch of dependence. This can happen even after successful performances. The cheers of the crowd don't fill the void of a lack of internal conviction and fulfillment in God's love for us. If you want to keep your emotional and spiritual center intact, you must learn to rest in the assurance that God loves you as you are, not only when you are performing or ministering. As Jesus taught us in Matthew 10:39, when you lose your life, you find it. In other words, when you give up the way you see yourself, you are free to see yourself the way God sees you. No matter how much music means to you, your true identity can only be found in Christ, and Christ alone.

I'm comforted by the fact that God doesn't need me operating in a musical capacity for me to be special to him. He has angelic beings that can sing and create music and praise non-stop. He gave me the blessing of music-making as a gift, not as a burden that chains me to a life spent searching for approval.

For some of you, this is not a problem. You're comfortable with who you are, and you have never struggled with an identity crisis over music. However, others of you have had sleepless nights, feeling lost as you tried to sort through your emotions following a show or a service. Once you flip your identity switch to 'performer', it can be hard to flip the switch back to being yourself. In Darlene Zschech's book, "Extravagant Worship", she refers to these feelings as "emotional fervor"[4]. In short, musicians can become so caught up in their passion for music that they lose the ability to maintain a God-centered perspective about their art.

It is important to note that while musical ability is a gift from God, it is not THE gift. God's greatest gift is salvation

---

[4]   Zschech, Darlene. 2001. Extravagant Worship: Holy, Holy, Holy is the Lord God Almighty who was, and is, and is to come. Bloomington: Bethany House Publishers.

through Christ and the presence of the Holy Spirit. Musical ability is simply a way that we can express our love and creativity. Even in the area of worship, music shouldn't be overemphasized. The modern church often contributes to this misconception by labeling the music portion of services as "praise and worship". In reality, worship can't be contained in a twenty minute set of songs. True worship involves every aspect of our lives. Music is only a *particular* way of expressing our worship, and perhaps even a *preferred* method for those of us that are gifted in this area. But God never pronounced music as the *preeminent* method of worshiping him, and therefore it is not the only part of our lives that matters. In fact, at one point in scripture, God explicitly *rejects* the worship songs of Israel (Amos 5:23). We are not simply gifted robots that must constantly perform in order to please God. God wants our hearts first. If we give him our hearts, he'll get our creativity.

In "The Gift of Art", G.E. Veith, Jr. comments, "For the artist as a person, faith in his or her art alone leads to spiritual death.[5]" When we worship our creativity more than the Creator, we are giving in to the idol of performance that is so prevalent in today's culture. We

---

[5] Veith, Jr., Gene Edward. 1983. *The gift of art: The place of the arts in Scripture.* Downers Grove: Intervarsity Press, p. 109.

must always be careful not to turn our music into the object of our affection rather than a tool to express our affections.

Answer these questions, then consider how you might need to change how you view your musical gifts.

- What talents and gifts do you have other than music?
- If you weren't a musician, what would you be?
- Did God only save you to perform for others?
- When are you happiest? Can you be happy when you're not performing?

If you really want to be able to handle the ups and downs of a music career, you must be able to imagine life without it while remaining true to yourself.

EXPLORE YOUR OTHER TALENTS AND ABILITIES

To be more than just a musician, you must have a healthy sense of what role music plays in your life and be able to take an honest assessment of its viability in your overall career. Of course, family and friends are often good counselors, but other times you will need an experienced music veteran to take you aside and explain what you can and cannot expect from your career. Many great musicians found their calling while doing other work, or by taking a break from music and recharging their batteries. In fact, because making music is often such a challenging career financially, you will often find amazing musicians who continue to work 9 to 5 jobs. They prefer the freedom to play when and where they want, without being limited by the need to gig constantly. It's important to remember that not everyone lives inside our musical bubble. While it is a worthy goal to be a full-time musician, there is no shame in maintaining your music as a secondary career while making life better for your family and pursuing other goals.

Personally, while music has provided much of my inspiration and financial support, I know that I have other interests and skills I can explore. I tutor middle and high school students in subjects like math, current events, and science, and I continue to hone my skills as a writer and blogger. If I decided to step away from music, I could go back to college to earn a master's degree in ministry or some other field of study. My point is that while music is a major part of my life, it is not my entire life. That reality keeps my mind fresh and open to all the possibilities that music affords me, knowing that it's a privilege and not a burden to be in this industry.

DEVELOP YOUR INNER LIFE

While maintaining your identity is its own reward, there is a musical benefit as well. The freedom and comfort that comes when you are not consumed by music alone actually increases your creativity and openness. You will feel the positive impact of your true self coming out of every note you sing or play. Herbie Hancock described this effect when giving a lecture at Harvard. A student asked him how he could develop a better touch at the keyboard. Hancock responded, "Develop your life." Our music is an outpouring of who we are on the inside, and usually, our best performances come when that internal identity is uninhibited by fear or self-doubt. The Bible puts it this way, "Where the spirit of the Lord is, there is liberty" (2 Corinthians 3:17). Liberty does not mean freedom from every rule and boundary. Rather, it is freedom to live, walk, and create as Christ intended us to. A musician who has fully accepted their identity in Christ is free to create and perform from a place of security, love, and joy.

This is why I believe that the Christian musician in the popular music industry is so important. As a secure, authentic believer who doesn't depend his or her musical identity alone, you encourage others in the industry to trust in something other than their talent or approval of others. For many artists, music is a god, and the approval of others is an altar. But if

God is the source and foundation of your life, your sense of security will make you stand out from the crowd. Your life can be a testimony that loving God does not stifle your creativity. Rather, your relationship with God frees you to be truly creative.

TAKE YOUR MUSIC IN NEW DIRECTIONS

As you grow personally and spiritually, you also must challenge yourself to reach new goals. Perhaps you dreamed of becoming a solo artist or touring the world, but you have not seen the fruition of that dream. If so, don't become frustrated while waiting on one dream to come true. Author and inspirational speaker Lynette Lewis once imparted this wisdom: while you wait on one dream, go pursue another one. Find new goals that you can work toward. Are there young musicians to mentor? New songs to write? Styles of music you've never explored? Never settle for just one version of your vision. Perhaps a delay in one area will redirect you into another aspect of music that you never would have considered otherwise.

Miles Davis famously said that if he ever played the music of a previous season of his life, it would kill him. Over the five decades of his career, he constantly changed his approach, despite those that criticized his choices. His refusal to avoid change helped to introduce entire new phases in jazz history, like bop jazz, cool jazz, free jazz, and fusion, until he finally played a tribute concert to his old music at the end of his career. It was his last recording before he died. While we aren't saying that playing a single style of music over a long period of time will have such a negative effect, it's also clear that many of the great musicians of our time have never been afraid to change, adapt, and reinvent their music.

How can a musician avoid becoming tied to the 'same old same old'? The best way is to constantly try new things. When you are open to trying new things, your creativity and passions are ignited.

Learn a new instrument. Once you have mastered your first instrument, you may forget how hard and how dedicated you had to be to learn it in the first place. Picking up a new instrument can re-awaken the desire you have to excel, open your ears to new possibilities, and connect you with other players that can become mentors and partners.

Study a new genre of music. Learning a style you have never tried – or even liked – can both make you appreciate the nuances of different eras and genres, and possibly give you a professional edge when looking for new opportunities. Clients and bands may need someone with expertise in a genre you have explored, which makes you even more valuable as a musician.

Connect with artists in other artistic disciplines. It is amazing how intertwined the fine arts are. Dance, sculpture, poetry, painting, and other fine arts all share common characteristics with music – application of form, skill and practice, discipline, expression of emotion, and many others. As you share with other artists and witness their approach to their craft, it can enlighten and inspire you to look at your craft in new and exciting ways.

Explore new techniques. Tiger Woods, arguably the best golfer of all time, has changed his swing several times over his career – changing even after using a certain swing won him several championships. You may be used to a certain approach to your instrument, but that approach may not be the only way. Being open to new techniques and approaches to your instrument can revolutionize and revitalize your performance and your productivity as a musician.

Attend conferences and workshops. As we talked about in "Visualizing Goals", conferences can awaken new ideas and connect you with other like-minded artists that can encourage and spark your creativity and passion for music.

Make new connections. Sometimes the right person can bring fresh insight and reveal a new direction for your music. Never be afraid to form new partnerships as you network with other artists. Over time, some of these new partners can shift your career and playing into a whole new direction that you never would have found on your own.

Mentor young musicians. Working with young musicians can inspire you with their energy, curiosity, and desire to learn. They are rarely jaded or frustrated with the system, and more importantly, you can help them to avoid the pitfalls and build a strong foundation in this business. This is especially important in music ministries, where we desperately need to nurture and build up the next generation of worship musicians.

We must never become satisfied with the music we made yesterday, even if it was the best music we thought we could make. There's always another level to reach! Are you willing to deal with the struggle to grow even when it's tough? That is what separates the casual musician from the true artist who creates for the love of the art.

ALLEN C. PAUL

Advice from the Pros

I believe the primary thing...is knowing where you were designed to thrive. There's an old adage that says 'bloom where you're planted'. Realize first and foremost that there is only one YOU and only one specific God-given purpose (in totality) for each of us on this earth. What I'm saying is every awesome, professional-grade musician won't expand past the four walls of their church! Some don't even have the desire...and some have tried many times and failed. And if that's you, you'll have to become comfortable with that. For most musicians in this realm, it will take lots of humility, time, and understanding where they thrive best in order to be O.K. with not being in the major spotlight. The good news is that these amazing individuals fall in the category of Bible spiritual gifts that, though unspoken in musical capacities, actually serve in the 'edification of the body'. (Eph. 4:12)

- Trent Phillips

God and Gigs

I understand the difficulty of reimagining your career and your approach to music. As I stated in my testimony, I found myself at a crossroads when I realized music was not fulfilling all my hopes and dreams. When my life revolved around music, my relationships became stale and my emotional balance was tenuous, at best. It was during that painful season of reevaluation that I learned what motivated me as a person, artist, and believer. I decided my life was solely about loving God, loving my family, and being true to my beliefs. As I ceased defining myself as only a musician, I became more comfortable in my own skin. Facing my own limitations allowed me to expand my limits and explore new goals and visions. You are reading the results of that season. Without that time of re-evaluation, this book never would have happened.

Musicians and artists, I want you to be free from the expectations that others place on you, and even those that you place on yourself. Letting go of your preconceptions can be scary, but seeing things differently is the key to success. Our success isn't determined by how many albums we sell or the size of the audiences we play for. God is the only one who knows the ultimate purpose for your gifts. It's up to you to trust and follow him even when your destination looks different than what you planned. Besides, God didn't create you only to be an artist. He created you to be loved by him and to love him back. Everything else is secondary.

Chapter Ten

Evangelize through your gift

My Lord, I should be sorry if I only entertained them. I wish to make them better.

- G.F. Handel

I've always considered myself a night person, but as I grow older, a good night's sleep becomes much more attractive. Most musicians view sleep as a luxury. We're accustomed to late night recording sessions and gigs that stretch into the early morning hours. There's something about the night that motivates us to display our talents. I believe there's a significant reason why musicians are often night creatures.

When the band takes a break on a gig, they'll usually find a place to relax, make calls or discuss the upcoming set with bandmates. I have a habit of taking stock of the audience as they wait for the next set. I like to get a feel for the people in the room. They are the ones who make it possible for us to have the career we have – people that spend hard earned money on entertainment and the arts. I often whisper a prayer of gratitude for every patron that supports my performances. However, I also know that within every crowd of cheering fans are people who haven't accepted Jesus as Savior. From the stage, there's no way for me to tell who is a believer and who is not, and I won't usually have an opportunity to meet or share my faith with those in the crowd. My heart sometimes hurts, knowing while these folks enjoy themselves in the late hours of the night, they will still be in spiritual darkness when the natural lights come back on.

Jesus calls himself the Light of the World, and later in the gospels he gives the church the same label. Yet, in many spiritually dark areas, there are no lights available. It seems when the neon lights begin glow in the city, the people carrying the Light of the World fade to black. When our light is absent, darkness prevails.

A musician's creativity shines brightly in any environment he or she enters, but this influence wasn't given to us so we can be seen and honored. Our light exists to reveal the true Light. God wants us to reveal his nature and his glory in all things and all circumstances, to guide others toward him through our conversation, conduct, and commitments. Jesus commands his followers to go into all the world making disciples, but few actually go where the world goes. Christian musicians have access to influential spaces in our culture that many in the church will never have. This means we have an awesome responsibility to carry the light of Christ into dark places while remaining both faithful and relevant.

For many, evangelism means picking up a Bible and marching from door to door, begging or barking at people to come to Jesus. While I pray you'll lead people to Christ through direct conversation, I'm speaking of evangelism in the sense of becoming a walking, talking representation of the gospel. Your gift will draw others to you. What will they find when they get close?

KEEP WORSHIP AS A PRIORITY

In order to influence others, you first must have a vibrant and growing relationship with God. This point bears repeating. In John 4, Jesus states that the Father is seeking worshippers that will worship in spirit and truth. This passage is familiar to praise leaders and church musicians. It's easy to see how authentic worship must be a priority for those that lead in our congregations. However, an attitude of worship isn't just important to those who serve on Sundays.

A worshipper is not just someone working in a church or lifting their hands in a service. I would define a worshipper as a person who consistently seeks God's presence and relies on his guidance. While some worshippers are musicians, not every musician is a worshipper. Musicians who don't seek the presence of God neglect the true source of their creative ability. It's not enough to have a familiarity with Christianity through your music. Knowing worship songs doesn't mean you know who you worship. In Philippians, Paul states that his greatest desire was to *know* Christ (Phil 3:10). Paul had myriad talents and abilities, but he didn't count any of them as important compared to his relationship with Jesus. Worshippers will never let their gifts get in the way of their pursuit of God.

You may be a skillful musician, but if you are not growing stronger and deeper as a worshipper, your music is like a 'sounding brass or clanging cymbal' (1 Corinthians 13). You may be considered influential by the world's standards, but without a daily habit of personal worship and prayer, your impact will be limited to applause and personal accolades. In order to represent Christ, you must be operating in the gifts of the Spirit, and the highest of those spiritual gifts is love. Your love of God is the core regarding your walk as a Christian musician. If you are traveling this journey without being rooted in God's love, your harvest will never produce the kind of fruit that will attract others to him. You have to remain rooted in the Vine, Jesus Christ, if you truly want to have an impact on the people around you.

I know this isn't easy. Those of us in popular music circles are constantly besieged by ideas and cultural waves that run counter to our beliefs. There have been times when I questioned my calling as a worshipper while working outside the church. The pressures and pulls of the professional music scene can be tough on the strongest believer. Performing takes something out of us emotionally. You may feel empty and unfulfilled when your creative tank is empty after non-worship activities, and you might question whether you are supposed to be giving so much energy outside of the house of God. However, I'm convinced that God restores and refreshes us as we wait on him, as Isaiah 40:31 states. If God has purposed you to be a musician, he will provide the resources, spiritually and physically, for you to accomplish the purpose he set out for you. Your identity as a child of God does not change based on where you are, and neither does the provision of God for your life. You have access to his power wherever you are as a child of God. Be assured, "God never changes his mind when he gives gifts or when he calls someone" (Rom 11:29, *GWV*).

KEEP GIVING OF YOURSELF

A popular verse among musicians and church goers in general is Proverbs 18:16: *A gift opens the way and ushers the giver into the presence of the great.*

Usually, in the King James Version, the first part of that verse is translated, "A man's gift makes room for him." When I've heard this verse used by musicians, they usually imply that the 'gift' in the verse refers to our talent. Supposedly, the gift of music is to open doors for us to play with the biggest and brightest of the industry. In other words, the purpose of my talent is to get me into the presence of great and influential people. However, upon further study, I found that this verse is not talking about talent as a gift at all.

The gift in this verse represents money, or the capacity of a person to give something in exchange for favor or position. It's clear from the text surrounding the verse that the writer is illustrating the power of gifts in both the positive and negative sense. A gift given as a manipulative device is a bribe. It does give a person access, but ends up becoming the giver's downfall when their true motives are discovered. On the other hand, those who give freely for the right reasons are often elevated and find themselves with much authority. Think of the gift the queen of Sheba gave to Solomon, or the tithe Abraham gave to the king of Salem. Each time, the gift created a space for elevation.

I believe the ultimate reason that God gives us the gift of music is to touch people with his love, and to show them the way to reach him through his Son, Jesus Christ. We're doubly blessed that we can make a living by sharing our talent, but what opens the door to true greatness is not how much money we make. It's how we share our gifts with others. Musicians who freely give their time, talent, and wisdom to others seem to attract success. We become great musicians when we embrace the spirit of giving.

I'm not saying that financial success isn't an important part of your career, and this isn't a plea to fill an offering plate. It's an appeal to your purpose. God blessed you with your talent, and now he waits to see if your attitude will be one of gratefulness and growth or of stinginess and stagnation. That's why I believe the greatest predictor of your success is your capacity to give. If you cannot learn to give artistically, financially, and physically, your time of greatness will either be short-lived or not happen at all. I repeat this for emphasis: Your attitude toward giving will determine your growth.

Why is giving so important? First, no matter what style of music you play, the initial purpose of music is to bring glory to God. Christ gave himself to die for our sins, and we as musicians have a gift to give away as well, in order to show others how grateful we are for the gift of salvation. If you don't know about this Gift, you can accept his gift freely right now by accepting Jesus' work on the cross on your behalf and asking him into your heart. For those of us who have done that, we now have a mandate to show others this Gift, and we have been given the powerful tool of music to help spread that truth. Does this mean every song we play must be all about Jesus? Of course not. We've already agreed that Christian plumbers, doctors, lawyers and every other profession show their faith not only by talking about Christ, but by the way they perform their work. As Colossians 3:17 states, "And whatever you do, whether in word or deed, do it all in the name of the Lord Jesus, giving thanks to God the Father through him ."

You can honor God and take his message into places that a preacher or pastor will never be invited to. You can attract others to Christ by your humility and excellence. You can be a light in a dark world by staying true to your faith and connected to the Word and to worship. God promises never to leave or forsake us, and I believe he will guide us even when we are tested in tough areas. You may be called to a spiritually foreign land for such a time as this, to be a major influence in areas that desperately need a light.

Advice from the Pros

Ministry is not based on where you are. It's what you do where you are.

- Greg Johnson, producer and keyboardist

There is another connection between gifts and the calling of an artist. I don't mean to stretch the Levitical analogy, but in Numbers 18:7, the Bible states a key phrase regarding the responsibilities of the Levites, which includes those that served in the creative arts. Aaron is told by God that the Levites (the priests) were a gift to him for the service of the ministry. While clearly these Levites were dedicated to ministerial functions, I believe this concept contains a kernel of truth even for the musician outside of the church. Music never ceases to be an act of service, and anytime a musician plays, his or her first concern is "who is going to hear this?" It's why we seek out an audience, and feel pretty crummy when we don't have anyone listening to us at a cocktail party or a concert. We become a discarded gift, unopened and ineffective in bringing anyone joy or fulfilling our purpose. Artists are built to be gifts to others. We must, therefore, acknowledge that a gift is meant to be given, and not meant to be a collection box for more gifts. A healthy, balanced musician must remain service-focused, even as he or she seeks out a livelihood and works hard to earn his income in a tough business. To become selfish and me-oriented is the first sign that a musician no longer understands the purpose of the giftedness he or she was blessed with.

Now, I can hear the musicians moaning in the background (Not you, the other person reading this book). "My church/ministry/gig is already asking me to give up a lot! I thought this book was about balancing work and family. Why should I be giving more when people are already taking so much?"

I hear you. A natural response of being a giver is a fear of giving out and giving in to everyone. I certainly don't recommend giving to everyone who simply asks for your time, talent, and treasure without first recognizing the reasoning behind the request. A great book on the topic of when to say "No" is *Boundaries: When to Say Yes, How to Say No to Take Control of Your Life* by Henry Cloud and John Townsend. However, I am recommending that every musician must recognize that by accepting the gift and benefits of artistry, you accepted the need and responsibility to serve others. The only way to get out of that responsibility is to give up your calling. Almost every artist I have encountered has stated, in some way, that they can't imagine life without their art – whether it is music, visual art, dance, etc. That's the natural and God-directed desire of the musician. We give away what we have received emotionally, spiritually, and artistically. Honor that desire, and you will find that God will make sure honor is returned to you in countless ways.

I can't tell you how many times I have been a gig, resting on a break with the band, and the conversation has turned to spiritual or family matters where I was asked to give the Christian viewpoint. I don't wear my faith as a badge at work, and many times people don't know my ministerial or church background when they call me for a job. However, by the end of the night, I usually end up talking to at least one musician about faith or family. I believe I'm positioned by God to bring comfort to hurting people at my gigs. There is much brokenness in the music industry, and each person on a bandstand desperately needs to know that they are loved by a God that wants the best for them. Being a servant-oriented musician in that environment opens the opportunity to 'pre-Christians' to find out just how God gives a creative artist peace with the Ultimate Creator. This is the practical application of Matthew 5:16, "Let your light shine before men, that they may see your good works, and glorify your Father which is in heaven." (KJV) In the original Greek, "works" in this sense is not just 'charitable deeds', but any work that is done in a spirit of beauty, honor, or excellence. We demonstrate the love of Christ by serving others. Doing so attracts our colleagues and our audiences to the true source of love, Jesus Christ.

> ## Advice from the Pros

Just like all the other members in church, we have to share our talent in and out of the church. It is as important as praising our Father in heaven. We have an obligation to our musician brothers out in the world. We don't have to say much. But our presence amongst them should be the catalyst in which a curiosity is born.

- **Dony Felix, bassist**

LET YOUR LIGHT SHINE

So far, I've focused on walking out your faith in the popular music field, where there's clearly a need for a Christian influence. If you only play for churches, you may think this chapter didn't apply to you. Not true. Sometimes, there are more unsaved people on the church platform than in the pews. Weekend after weekend, in churches all over the world, musicians, singers, and leaders play, sing, and lead solely on the strength of their talent. They appear to be authentic, but they have no relationship with the God they sing and play for.

Evangelism starts at home. We should let the light of Christ shine everywhere we go, even among our peers who think of worship as just another gig. We need musicians in our churches that understand the gift they have is more than a musical one, but a "treasure in jars of clay," as stated in 2 Corinthians 4:7.

I understand that it can be awkward to question the validity of someone's faith. It's not a good idea to judge a fellow musician's salvation, unless of course they are willing to share their spiritual journey honestly with you. The best way to help develop more authentic music ministry at your church is to become a more dedicated worshipper yourself. This has much less to do with music and more to do with a spiritual hunger and thirst to know God intimately. As artists, we have a God-given sensitivity to mood and atmosphere that can often touch people's lives with just a word or a note. That same sensitivity must be utilized when we search after God's heart and his will. His calling on our lives can only be discerned through time with him, reaching his word, and being open to his voice. Maybe this isn't something you have done before. Let me assure you that you haven't begun to scratch the surface of your ability and anointing until you have sought the Lord's direction.

When others in your music ministry witness your authenticity in seeking God's heart, only two things can happen. Either they will reject or misinterpret your passion or they will be inspired by it. Don't be discouraged if others don't understand your drive to be a God-chaser. Light always reveals darkness, and those who don't want to be exposed will often criticize those who are reflecting God's glory. However, those inspired by your love of God will emulate you and connect with you. Together, you can take your music ministry to a deeper level of spiritual intimacy that goes far beyond the music you play every weekend.

DON'T BE DISCOURAGED

Music ministry seems to be a magnet for conflict in many churches. Whether revealed through pride, ungodly relationships, jealousy, power grabs, or pettiness, all the issues common to music departments stem from a breakdown of relationship. When there is unresolved conflict in the music ministry, the anointing and unity that is required for real spiritual connection is restricted. People in the congregation may not know what is going on, but everyone can sense the tension. Sooner or later, the lack of real relationship will reveal itself in the attitude of the musicians and the quality of worship will decline.

Jesus himself told us without him, we can't do anything. Nothing of eternal significance is created when we are apart from him. Our songs mean nothing, our chords mean nothing, and our talent is a brash and empty sound that changes nothing. This cancer of disconnection can spread through your life if you put more faith in people and position than in Christ. Before long, the relationship between you and God may become frail, and soon after, your godly relationships may begin to falter. Instead of planting seeds of love, worship, and devotion in the local church, musicians who are relationally broken plant the enemy's crops. This is why music ministries become infected with dissension, greed, envy, and all the other desires of the flesh listed in Galatians 5:19-20. When we're damaged by division in our churches, our witness to the world has no power.

The division that damages our testimony often shows up in conflicts with our ministry leaders. A musician who has no respect for the God they serve will not have respect for the authority that God set up within the local church, and certainly not within a music ministry. This is why the battle of wills between music ministry leaders and musicians always seems to center around authority. A musician who understands their gift belongs to God will be able to handle the authority placed in the hands of a pastor or worship minister. However, musicians who don't honor God as the source of their gift tend to reject spiritual leadership. These musicians might respect a director in their other performances, but within the church, they don't honor the high value God places submitting to authority.

If you have noticed this problem in your own life, you need to remember the warning of Proverbs 16:18; *pride goes before destruction, and a haughty spirit before a fall.* Whether or not you are a leader outside a church, you must be willing to accept the leadership direction that the pastor of the house has set up. Scripture clearly states this principle in 1 Thessalonians 5:12 (NLT); *Dear brothers and sisters, honor those who are your leaders in the Lord's work.*

The only way a music ministry can survive the constant battle between the darkness of pride and ego and the light of Christ is to promote the 'ministry of reconciliation' (2 Cor. 5:18). This is not a musical skill. It is a spiritual attribute that every Christian must practice. Every music ministry deals with complaints and competition at some point. But those that survive and grow are those with musicians who respect God's order and the leadership of the church. These attributes don't come from practice. They come from time in the Word, and they are honed and made effective from rubbing shoulders with those who are not always lovable or professional. In other words, we build our faith when we commit to loving others in the midst of difficult situations.

That's the heart of evangelism – demonstrating the love of God in a tangible way that draws people to him. Evangelism doesn't stop on the church platform, but it can start there.

CONCLUSION

Musicians that understand their primary purpose will be confident in their calling even when criticized by those who may not understand. They will be teachable, but also apt to teach and help others in their ministry to aspire to the high-calling that their gift demands. They will always point to Christ as their guide and their inspiration to create, instead of using their gift as a crutch for real relationship or a feather in their cap for showmanship. To evangelize the lost is the primary reason the church exists, and we have a role to play in this work.

Levites in Moses' day were servants of the highest order. They were given a job and a ministry at the same time; their work was worship, and they worshipped through their work. In the same way, Christian musicians in this day and age can bring glory to God through their conduct and character in places few others will have the chance to influence. Jesus taught that the greatest position in the Kingdom was that of a servant. You will only reach your highest potential when you approach your work as a musician with a servant's heart.

And so we come full circle in the S.E.R.V.I.C.E. model. We began with the conflicts between the practice of music ministry and the practicality of the music business, but there really is no division between the two. In every situation, you are called to serve. Serve God and treat others with love, honor, respect, and excellence, knowing that doing so brings honor and glory to the Father of all. I pray that your music, and more importantly your life, is a beacon of light to all who seek to know Jesus in a real way. I implore you to be prayerful and faithful as you work as a Christian musician. Everywhere you go, God can and will prepare the way for you, so that you can love him, love your music and love his people.

APPENDIX

Recommended Resources

The following books were referenced or were helpful in the writing of God and Gigs. I encourage you to read them to further develop your life and career skills.

CREATIVE AND ARTISTIC DEVELOPMENT

1. The Artisan Soul: Creating Your Life into a Work of Art, By Erwin Raphael McManus, ISBN 978-0062270290
2. The War of Art: Break Through the Blocks and Win Your Inner Creative Battles, by Steven Pressfield, ISBN 978-1936891023

3. The Gift of Art: The place of the arts in Scripture, by Gene Edward Veith, ISBN 978-0877848134

Music Ministry and Spiritual Development

4. Excellence in Worship: Should Church Musicians Be Paid?, by Darrell Alexander, ISBN 978-1412060615
5. Extravagant Worship: Holy, Holy, Holy is the Lord God Almighty who was, who is, and is to come, by Darlene Zschech, ISBN 978-0764200526
6. From Performance to Praise: Moving Music Ministry to the Next Level, by Joe Pace, ISBN 978-0971270183

Personal Growth and Relationship Guidance

7. The Peacemaker: A Biblical Guide to Resolving Personal Conflict, by Ken Sande, ISBN 978-0801064852

8. Boundaries: When to Say Yes, How to Say No to Take Control of Your Life, by Henry Cloud and John Townsend, ISBN 978-0310247456

Music Industry and Career Advice

9. The Savvy Musician: Building a Career, Earning a Living & Making a Difference, by David Cutler, ISBN 978-0982307502
10. The Musician's Way: A Guide to Practice, Performance, and Wellness, by Gerald Klickstein, ISBN 978-0195343137

For more resources, encouragement and advice for musicians and artists, visit

GodandGigs.com

INDEX

A

accountability, 43, 99
advertising, 136
Advice from the Pros
    Bennett, Dwayne 114
    Dentley, Kristian 56, 62, 123
    Felix, Dony 185
    Johnson, Greg 182
    Phillips, Trent 79, 172
    Russo, Victor 79
amateur, 88
approval, 91, 128, 136, 163, 167
Artist
    accountability groups, 32
    calling of, 10, 182-184
    gospel, 15
    growth of, 168-173
    married, 42
    need for prayer, 71-72
    parenting as an, 53-60
    priorities of, 134
    rap, 15
    role in ministry, 14
    selfishness of, 125
    touring, 48
    using influence, 21-22
    (see also: influence)
attire, 151
attitude, 22, 25, 30, 69, 104, 188
    confident, 137-138
    giving, 180
    humble, 141
    negative, 125
    prideful, 122, 136
    professional, 115–116
    worshipping, 176

authenticity, 42 - 43, 161 - 162, 187
authority, 44 - 45, 68, 114, 120, 179, 188 - 189

B

balance, 12, 27, 62, 71, 112, 173
Bennett, Dwayne 92, 114
Bible, 34, 36, 66 - 68, 125
  reading, 72-78
  studies, 37, 75-76

boundaries, 183, 194
Bowens, Parris 96 - 106
brand, 4, 96, 136, 139, 151
business, 6, 107, 151

C

Calling, 10, 159
Career, 81, 194
Children, 52, 54, 55
Church, 24, 30, 91, 111, 193
Church Musicians, 9, 20, 115, 176
circles, 61, 121, 122, 136, 178
cliques, 122
commitment, 16, 70, 83, 113, 145
  financial, 148
  to career paths, 90-91
  to church, 31, 34, 36
  to family, 63
  to spouse, 41, 46
Communication, 112, 145
Conflict, 193
congregation, 15, 17, 29, 79, 187
consistency, 108, 121
contract, 111
Conversations with the Pros, 11, 47, 57, 92
  Bowens, Parris 96
  Velandia, Camilo 47
  Dentley, Khristian 56, 62, 123
  Dawkins, James 144
  Bennett, Dwayne 92
  Murphy, Stephane and Lavie 57
creativity, 20, 175

D

Dawkins, James 144
Davis, Miles 139, 168
debt, 132, 150, 151

decisions, 39, 43, 100, 148
    career, 83, 94, 148
    creative, 70, 139
    godly, 31, 73
    in marriage, 41-43
    in vision statement, 131
    parenting, 60
    to play secular music, 21
Dentley, Kristian 56, 62, 123
divorce, 30, 40

E

education, 15, 144
Ellington, Duke 40
employers, 95
Equipment, 133
eternal, 64, 126, 188
Evangelism, 186, 190

F

Facebook, 8, 135
faith, 18
    Biblical examples, 68
    in creativity alone,
    in S.E.R.V.I.C.E model, 22
    maintaining, 13-15, 92 145-46
    of Namaan, 68
    setting goals, 128-135
    sharing, 181, 184-85
    struggling with, 32
Faithfulness, 50, 123
Fame, 89
Family, 95, 103, 133
fear, 36, 39, 93, 97-99, 100, 138, 167, 183
Felix, Dony 185
finances, 150
freelance, 157
freelancer, 8
friendship, 50-51

G

Gift, 164, 180, 193
giving, 36, 76, 164, 167,
    affected by debt, 150
    attitude of, 178-83
    credit for talent, 76
    goals, 128, 170

Gospel, 154

H

Hancock, Herbie 167
Holy Spirit, 19, 77, 100 - 101, 103-05, 164
husband, 32, 41 - 42, 56 - 57, 62, 102, 131

I

identity, 84, 90, 139, 152, 161-163, 167, 178
Image, 151
influence, 35, 44, 69
- of Christ, 9
- on others, 14, 21-22, 68, 79, 181
- of the church, 28
- among musicians, 102
- on culture, 141, 175-177, 190
- in education, 153
- in music ministry, 185

inspire, 73, 85, 86, 138, 170, 171, 187
integrity, 108, 111, 114, 120, 1

J

Jesus
- in song lyrics, 21
- Gospel of, 34, 135
- authority of, 44
- teachings of, 64, 85, 162, 188, 188, 190
- connection to, 66
- inner circle, 122
- at wedding of Cana,
- as Savior, 175, 179-80
- light of the World, 175
- command to evangelize, 175-77, 191

Johnson, Greg 182

K

Kingdom, 106, 135, 190

L

Lavie, 57
Levites, 13- 14, 182, 190
Lindsey, Aaron 72, 131
Love
- of music, 13, 46, 53, 60, 66, 86, 171

in songs, 43
in church families, 29-30, 34, 36, 188
in marriage, 39, 42, 48
in friendships, 50
of God, 76, 162, 173, 177-79, 184, 187, 190-91
of teaching, 102
expressive 164, 167

M

marriage, 38 - 46, 50 - 51, 57, 103, 105
mindset, 115, 140, 146, 162
minister, 79, 88, 100, 103, 158, 161, 189
of music, 10, 17-18, 54, 144
motivation, 86, 87, 89
Murphy, Stephane 57
Music ministry, 187
musicianship, 87, 90

P

partnership, 111, 112, 118, 124, 170

passions, 85, 86, 90, 169
pastor, 11, 24 - 25, 32 - 35, 97, 100, 111 - 112, 188 – 189
Phillips, Trent 79, 172
popular music, 12, 92, 144, 145, 154, 167, 178, 185
practice, 194
prayer, 70, 131
preparation, 110
presentation, 109
pride, 136
priorities, 82, 161
professional, 88, 89, 133
professionalism, 70, 97, 108, 151
promotion, 18, 54, 135, 136, 151, 152
punctuality, 110, 120

R

recording, 57, 91, 151
relationships, 35
reputation, 108 -09, 114, 124, 125, 142
resources, 192
respect, 22, 107, 113

S

scheduling, 20, 112
Scripture, 113, 164, 189, 193
secular, 10
single, 43, 45, 138, 169
skill, 147
spirit, 21, 100, 102, 103, 136, 177
spouse, 38
stability, 28, 29, 35, 59, 160
style, 87, 115 - 18, 152, 155, 168-69, 180
success, 11, 100, 102, 137-38, 173, 180
    critical areas, 27
    dreams of, 56, 129
    priorities, 64
    desires for, 71—72, 125-129
    motivation, 89
    networking for, 140-143

T

talent, 188
taxes, 150
technology, 49, 73, 74, 75, 130, 154
temptations, 32, 43, 44
touring, 49
trust, 119

V

Velandia, Camilo 47
vision, 83, 122, 124, 129-33, 135-43, 168, 173
volunteer, 19, 27, 36, 88, 89

W

website, 138, 151, 152

wife, 38-39, 41, 44, 47-49, 52, 58, 96, 103-05, 131
Worship, 95, 154, 163, 193

www.ingramcontent.com/pod-product-compliance
Lightning Source LLC
Chambersburg PA
CBHW020613300426
44113CB00007B/631